TIPTOEING IN & OUT

TANKA POETRY

Fabrizio Frosini
Poets Unite Worldwide

Fabrizio Frosini

TIPTOEING IN & OUT

Tanka Poetry

Fabrizio Frosini & Poets Unite Worldwide

TANKA by

Anna Banasiak
Simon J. Daniel
Sheryl Deane
Fabrizio Frosini
Nicholas Gill
Carlo Gomez
Birgitta Abimbola Heikka
Lidia Hristeva
Nadeem Ishaque
Joji Varghese Kuncheria
Konstantinos Lagos
Aron Lelei
Mj Lemon
Geeta Radhakrishna Menon
Valsa George Nedumthallil
Mohammed Asim Nehal
Namita Rani Panda
Annette Potgieter
Udaya R. Tennakoon
Hans Van Rostenberghe
Steven Vogel
Caroline Watsham
Somayeh Zare

Editorial Project by
Fabrizio Frosini

Editorial Board
Fabrizio Frosini, Annette Potgieter

Tiptoeing In & Out

Tanka Poetry

Fabrizio Frosini and Poets Unite Worldwide

Independently Published by Fabrizio Frosini

ISBN: 9798424436260

Anthology of poetry — Tanka by:

Anna Banasiak, Simon J. Daniel, Sheryl Deane, Fabrizio Frosini, Nicholas Gill, Carlo Gomez, Birgitta Abimbola Heikka, Lidia Hristeva, Nadeem Ishaque, Joji Varghese Kuncheria, Konstantinos Lagos, Aron Lelei , Mj Lemon, Geeta Radhakrishna Menon, Valsa George Nedumthallil, Mohammed Asim Nehal, Namita Rani Panda, Annette Potgieter, Udaya R. Tennakoon, Hans Van Rostenberghe, Steven Vogel, Caroline Watsham, Somayeh Zare

Editorial project by Fabrizio Frosini

Cover: image from Pixabay.com, used under Creative Commons CC0

this body
grown fragile, floating,
a reed cut from its roots...
if a stream would ask me
to follow, I'd go, I think

Ono no Komachi (821?-880?)

Table of Contents

lying alone,
my black hair tangled,
uncombed,
I long for the one
who touched it first

Izumi Shikibu (979?-1033?)

OPENING NOTE & ACKNOWLEDGMENTS

This book, which features more than three hundred original tanka, never published before, is devoted entirely to Tanka poetry and joins the three previous collections of Haiku and Senryū published by Poets Unite Worldwide [§]

Tanka —a word that means *short poem*, or *short song*— being a short lyric poem, is usually emotional, opinionated, even sensual. Intensity and intimacy derive from the direct expression of emotions, or through implications, suggestions, and nuances.

This collection consists of **321 Tanka**, written by twenty-three poets, and since each of them experiences their emotions with different tones and shades, these differences can be perceived in the poems by an attentive reader. I therefore chose **53** tanka (*out of 321*) to build **sequences**, according to 4 main themes: a way to propose a different reading, which can involve the reader even more.

In the 'Addendum' section the reader can also find some in-depth pages on Tanka poetry — including a short essay, taken from one of our previous publications, written by the late Daniel J. Brick (its title is, "*Ancient Japanese Poetry*")

Acknowledgments

My heartfelt thanks to All the Poets who contributed their tanka to this Anthology. I also wish to express my gratitude to Annette Potgieter for her invaluable help as co-editor of this volume.

Enjoy the book

(*Fabrizio Frosini, Firenze, February 2022*)

(§) Anthologies by PUW:

- 'Seasons of the Fleeting World – Writing Haiku'
- 'Moments of Lightness – Haiku & Tanka'
- 'Born on a Full Moon — Senryū'

My personal collections:

- «A Season for Everyone – Tanka Poetry»
- «Evanescence of the Floating World – Haiku
- «KARUMI – Haiku & Tanka

all night long

we kept the brushwood burning

in my humble hut

the words that we exchanged

I shall never forget

Jakuren (1139–1202)

TANKA

BY AUTHOR

ANNA BANASIAK

1.

morning has broken
like a palette of colours
it's good to taste life
drinking coffee in silence
in the lonely life cafe

2.

listening to jazz
I find the world dancing and
problems disappear...
thoughts are melting in music
in a cosy room of dreams

3.

engulfed in terror
lives were interrupted and
dreams left in rubble

      in the valley of despair
      memory and grief remains

9/11 Anniversary

(Anna Banasiak, Poland)

SIMON J. DANIEL

1.

deer-spotting it's called —

as I walk with my cousin
Scamp, the dog, leads us —

all of a sudden o'er there
beautiful ornate antlers

2.

far out the window
I peer at the darkness still
what's there or who's there?

darkness paves the way for light
and I discern an image

3.

when in a bus
travelling somewhere out there
I chanced upon them:

a mother in a torn veil
the daughter in finery!

4.

I came to a halt
'coz the traffic light turned red
right in front of me

     a vision like it's ne'er been:
     my Lord — His eyes so tranquil!

5.

after all the noise
din and the hullaballoo
mom only said — God
    let the scorpion pick on
    me and spare my children!

Author's note:
"It refers to Nissim Ezekiel's The Night of the Scorpion."

(Simon J. Daniel, India)

SHERYL DEANE

1.

when the seething sea
swallows the molten rock
its waters sizzle...
    how she clutches her ears when
    the volcano spews fire!

2.

the frozen mountains
glitter silver and white
in the distance...
    oh, to live one minute more
    and follow a snowflake's path!

3.
a world of lilies
under an old wooden bridge
floats etched in her soul —
an imaginary world
but it lives on her palette

(Sheryl Deane, South Africa)

FABRIZIO FROSINI

1.

you two smiling —
that made the day lighter
even for me, here

    then a thought crossed my mind:
        space-time is a boundary...

———————
(dedicated to A. & W.)

2.

the olive oil stain
spilled on the tablecloth
has a face shape;
I look in the mirror
to compare it to mine

3.

they embrace
and flow together as one
the two skaters:
"you and me?" your words in red
on a forty-year-old card

4.

her red ribbon lands
gracefully on my shoulder
as I hear her laugh...

nostalgically walking
down the memory lane

5.

even after years
in all the faces I meet
I always see yours...

the sheer oddities of this
moody old poet — you'd say

6.

every now and then
in the darkness of the mind
a voice sings her name

almost a comfort and yet
a guilt that keeps haunting me

7.

we liked making love
under the star-studded sky —

your eyes too were stars...

we were young and with minds full
of plans — how naive we were!

8.

countless days we spent
embracing each other
with joyful passion;

but we knew: *all that is—ends*
whether you want it or not

9.

early autumn rains
always bring old memories
and nostalgia:
the sweetness of your bright smile
the joy that your eyes conveyed

10.

I close my eyes
delving in memories
and breathe deeply...

the scent of your body
is still overwhelming

11.

our evolutions
under a clear evening sky
with the starlings —

we dance in unison, with
geometric perfection

12.

your hair's on my face
and your light breath's a sweet breeze
on my neck...

    quietly we fell asleep
        each of us in our own dreams

13.

"ten thousand years
like the turtle's life span
loom over me!"

she kept texting even though
I was just five minutes late

Author's note:
10,000 years: the lifespan of the "spiritual turtle" in ancient Chinese mythology.

14.

she asked me
"how long have you been waiting?"
and sent me a kiss —

since when did I start waiting
for her? since forever

15.
if only I had
a magic wand for an hour
I would change my world...

she told me one autumn night
many years ago — and then...

16.
I shared with her
thoughts that I should have kept
to myself —
if now she is suffering
the fault is mine, entirely

17.

when I saw her...

a far distant memory
awakens — but...

did it happen for real
or was I just daydreaming?

18.

was it worth the wait?

my unrequited love asks
on my grave...

when will I be given
a night free from such dumb dreams?

19.
lost time is lost
and nothing lasts forever

we tell each other —

the weird shadow of the night
lengthens over both of us

20.
loneliness has
many faces and deep hues
you once told me —
now I stand in this twilight
and paint all its colors

21.

I feel life sinking
as I watch the setting sun
sink into the see...

"you won't be here for long"
a voice from within says

22.

disturbed by the glare
I take my eyes away
from the world —
an eerie afterglow
remains etched in the mind

23.

in the sand I write
in hardly worked out verse
meaningless poems

they can be read both ways:
as jokes or symptoms of age

24.

ah, poetry...

as an inseparable
aspect of life...

    which offers no definite
    answers to life itself

25.

sharp and sheer
is the voice of the soul
whenever she speaks —
but the meaning of those words
remains alien to my ears

26.

where to find
a silent, unknown place
where to rest...
is it somewhere
in the space of the mind?

27.

on the willow
at the end of the garden
a cuckoo...
with full awareness
I'm waiting for darkness

28.

despite everything
the path towards the end
is never sad

as long as the end is near
and that it does not leave streaks

29.

alone

after I lost my own
world...

> I sail through the sheer
> emptiness of my mind

~*~

30.

the future
is terra incognita,
yet you can *see* it?

> ah, delusions arise from
> our psyche's fragility!

31.

you say they control
the minds of the masses
through a vaccine?

you'd rather get sick and die
than get vaccinated — fool!

32.

lost to QAnon
he believes the democrats
control people's minds

in that deadly online cult
he's lost control of himself

33.

too many believe
in conspiracy theories
artfully constructed...

    a psychological test
        to prove our stupidity?

34.

perusing the text
I find something to refute
since it is untrue

    "a false story, yes" he says
    "but it's absolutely cool!"

35.

it takes so little
to tarnish decades of good
reputation...

and when you are not guilty
the pain is devastating

36.
heaven and hell do
coexist in the world and
they fight within us...

in my endless nights without
stars or hope your words resound

37.
we are always
at each other's throats
seeking revenge...
yet we cannot explain why
we hate each other so much

38.
as I got older
I lost my initial faith
in humans —

   pray to find it, you now say,
      but to whom should I pray?

39.
in a wheelbarrow
the toddler smiles at the world —
ravishing picture

   will he still be so smiling
   after thirty years or so?

40.

they did not commit
anything wrong, yet they brace
for retribution —

who are the culprits now
but those who broke their promise?

Afghanistan, August 15, 2021.

41.

twenty years have passed
but the sorrow doesn't end
for those who bear it...
in a world so divided
their names are spoken once more

9/11 Anniversary — 2,977 died on this day 20 years ago (2001).

42.

october scenes:

two kids climb the steep hillside,
nimble as ferrets;

the old man in a wheelchair
slowly adjusts his face mask

43.

"lead by example
like your great president does"

    we were told

then through the news we learned:
our president was corrupt!

44.

beyond their pretense
what matters are the facts
seen by all —

and yet those who seek power
at all costs stop at nothing!

_____

January 6th Anniversary: 1 year after the Capitol attack (1/6/2021).

45.

lies and cynical
disinformation came first
then guiltless blood...

the damned puppeteer laughs
sardonically — in hell

_____

Ukraine, February 2022.

46.

with tanks and missiles
the macabre dance starts and
evil rejoices —

    he plays the role of a god
    as mad as the worst devil

Ukraine, February 2022 — Putin's destabilizing plans.

47.

he laughs, sobs, screams like
he's running a marathon
through feelings...
the emotional response
of an emotional kid

48.

schadenfreude:

with his foot in the pit
the fool laughs...

but even if he is rich
he can't escape destiny

Author's note:
Schadenfreude: "pleasure caused by the misfortune of others."

49.

insensitive world!
yet you say that there are still
beautiful people...

are you heralding perhaps
a world of resurgent dreams?

50.

for good or bad
his oddities are truly
intriguing...

this moody old poet knew
how to captivate readers

~*~

51.

deep night — its small sounds
fall into an odd rhythm
of silence

 where past and present mingle
 with the ghost of the future

52.

the owl is howling...

why should owls be harbingers
of bad omens?

 although birds of darkness,
 the night is full of beauties

53.

mesmerizing lights
on the gloomy ocean floor
reveal themselves:
living lights for which darkness
is their only universe

54.

cries of birds
from the evergreen grove
in the moonlight

in the sky pierced by cries
the lights of a thousand stars

55.
they filled every space
even those unsuitable
for nesting—the birds...

    yet in the world's formula
    everything has its own place

56.
with fluid movements
she performs her ballet
in the fairy blue:
white-dark wings sway back and forth
in flight — ah, the humpback whale!

57.
Kruger park —
a lone dozing lycaon
lying on a path...

    dreaming of its pack chasing
    great kudus to exhaustion?

58.
how worldly you are...

says the look in his eyes
from the tv screen —

    the silverback turns and goes
        a step towards extinction?

———————
Author's note:
'Silverback': any mature male mountain gorilla (aged 12 years or older).

59.

sloping down southwards
it forms a gentle valley,
the big mountain —

my stream of thoughts seems to flow
like a bright brook down the slope

60.

from up here
the beguiling landscape
takes my breath away

like snakes rivers slice through lands
you'd say untouched—but are not

61.

"vanishing salmon..."
you hear the old man say
in a hoarse voice

    but you don't realize it's
    your world that's fading away

62.

only a few fish
in the murky blue waters
of the lake —
they swim without knowing
they are the last to live there

63.

with loud roars
mighty centuries-old oaks
fall to the ground —

on Earth Day, heavy steel-beasts
roam the gutted forest

Author's note:
Earth Day is an annual event held on April 22nd to support environmental protection.

64.

three hundred years old:
I look at the fallen tree
in deep dejection —

I still don't understand
the true meaning of life

65.

sentient mammals
we say we are, and should be,
but we are not:
we are a mortal danger
to life on earth — to all kinds!

66.

deceptively
inside the cage of life
we're shown an exit —

    across turbulent waters
    our imagination swims

67.

in Glasgow puppets
pulled by tarry threads spoke of
solemn commitments...
how to save the world from those
who just want to exploit it?

COP26: the 26th UN Climate Change conference, Glasgow (Nov. 2021).

68.

deforestation —
the Amazon rainforest
is disappearing...
yet Bolsonaro pledges
to ending it in ten years!

Author's note:
In the Amazon, deforestation accelerated under Brazilian President Jair Bolsonaro: 13,235 sq km (5110 sq miles) of rainforest were lost in 2020 — an increase of 22% in one year, and the highest amount since 2006.

69.

unbearable life —
the sea level rises
as ice sheets melt:
our oceanfront home is now
an island about to drown

70.

onto the village
the atmospheric river
has discharged a lake

water and mud I glimpse
where old houses used to be

71.
relentlessly
we try to gild the lily
needlessly —
we kill and destroy instead
still unnecessarily

Author's note:
"Gilding the Lily": spoiling something that is already beautiful or perfect by trying to improve it or by praising it too highly.

72.
the paulownia
I would choose as a symbol
for the New Year —
a wonderfully wise tree
that can bear the greatest gifts

73.

I would plant a fir —
one for each day of the year
if I had the chance...

a grove: the abode of souls
made of music and pure light

74.

ah, how I wither
facing the challenges
of life!

    the sturdy sheep keep grazing
    in the windy winter field

75.

eight are the legs
of the spider patiently
waiting for the breeze —

while I struggle to walk
he'll soon fly with the wind

76.

dust — after gas, the
most common ingredient
in the universe...
the smallest granules — strings of
molecules — and we are born!

77.

ah, if the fragments
by which we somehow exist
were mobile:
we could tear them down and
reassemble them at will!

78.

alone in this world,
abandoned to ourselves,
though we didn't ask...

ah, this impassible,
unconcerned universe!

79.

trapped in a lie
we lay down on a warm dream
ready to vanish...

    imaginary are we
        made of hidden quark flavors

80.

beyond the edge
the deepest mystery looms:
end of the voyage?

but the cosmos of the mind
has no edges — no limits

(*Fabrizio Frosini, Italy*)

NICHOLAS GILL

1.

a wise man I dreamed
showed me a clear forest path
through my tangling thoughts...
but I'm travel weary
and no moon lights the dark wood

2.

they gave me this life
in an urban prison camp
and my soul rebelled...
I fled into my deep self
and lost my way to the world

3.

death, my constant friend,
you have patiently called me
across life's wide stream —
the inexplicable dream
from which we yearn to awake

4.

I almost drowned as
a child in a cold river:

my teacher saved me —

in return for my music
he's gone and the music too

(*Nicholas Gill, UK*)

CARLO C. GOMEZ

1.

the city lights shine
they shine soft as church candles
religiously so

    in the glow we know so well
    we reach for eternity

2.

the missing chess piece
I suspect is in her hand
concealed for triumph

    all part of the evening's fun
    her hidden scheme against me

3.

the flight of a kite
taken by the reckless wind
lost in distant clouds

    and here the fall of her hair
    tethers my mind to the sky

4.

another green world
and another yellow sun...

    carbon based life forms!

disposable and dead
as alkaline batteries

5.

no more rats they said
but pied piper wasn't paid...

    he lured the kids out!

our hearts are now cleaved and
these silent streets bereaved

(*Carlo C. Gomez, USA*)

BIRGITTA ABIMBOLA HEIKKA

1.

what a valley!
and perched high up the garden!
ah, my mouth waters...

neapolitan ice cream
in the garden palatial

2.

behind the girls' halls
the forest sublime sprawls large
under the sun —

banana leaves shade us
as we pick up kola-nuts

3.

in multitudes
they come crawling up my skirt—
the stinging ants...

    I smash them with my shoes
    but their bites burn dearly

4.

no enjoyment
from playing with my doll
stiff as a baseball —

I bounced it off the wall
'till it hit me in the eye

5.

slim, tall and regal
in straight lines like sentries stand
rows of rubber trees —

their milk pours into pails
held by shiny white sashes

6.

lumps of giant hail
like falling diamonds
hit my car —

a surprise that blinded me:
was it the end of the world?

7.

into the mouth
of the bight he entered
and disappeared...

ah, those who don't heed the sign
"do not swim farther"!

8.

he saw the plane
as a means to freedom
and clung to its wing...

the boy like a bird shot down
from the distant sky fell

9.

there is emptiness
in eyes too young for despair,
children of Haiti —

the earth quakes beneath their feet
as if it were their sworn foe

10.

covetousness —
a devil passed me by
and I knew evil...

he tore off the ear lobes
of a girl with gold earrings

(*Birgitta Abimbola Heikka, USA*)

LIDIA HRISTEVA

1.

a still loving heart
never waves a sad goodbye
to a youth long gone —
age adds more depth to it
to rejuvenate its thrill

2.

this sadness of mine...
such human heart's enemy
changes its colour
    never comes in white only
    some days it is black emptiness

3.

now is the time
to change this harsh world into
a loving one
or the world will change your soul
into a wandering wolf

4.

alas, you dim stars!
no words capture the feeling
of sheer loneliness —

darkness anchors the heart while
the soul grows numb in silence

5.

fulfil a life dream?
how hollow a fantasy
to seek happiness...
this heartless planet filled with
sheer human indifference

6.

the fragrance of spring
is your velvety lips
kissing a blossom...
my first kiss is still with me
though I forgot how to kiss

7.

a crescent rainbow
colours the summer sky
after the rainfall —
my weary heart leaps in joy:
a silent gleeful feeling

8.

my heart has been a
long-term repository
for your own pain...
through my soul's awareness
I can feel the scars you left

9.

your long-enchained love
needs a loose and fresh breath
to get happiness —
I'll cut the entanglement
to make you happy again

10.

you —
who loved me beyond lust
and desire...
how deeply bonded our souls
are, my dream lover

11.

kindness
has no firm boundaries
you know —
it will be the salvation
of your hateful heart

12.

this world
is drowning in a fog
of vanities...
the existential self
is emptied of purpose

13.

even the glad heart
holds sorrowful memories
deep inside —
their relics are sacred nests
where a rebirth can happen

14.

life is nothing but
a curious form of art
that can storm at times:
be it a hurricane
or just love and blessing

15.

don't adjust your heart
to a place you don't belong:
rebel injustice!
before it spoils what you aren't
but they think you are

16.

the passion of love
our innocent youth inhaled
and made its own...
we keep carrying it
throughout our life as sinners

17.

the soft sea breeze
brings me your warm caress
this night —
it is a comfort to heart
and mind haunted by nightmare

18.

how about your love
if you fear a lifetime
commitment?
only doubtful hearts and mind
are content with raw flings

19.

words are black ashes
that cannot paint the loss
of a loved one —
what is life preparing now?
beauty is so despondent

20.

hanging on a tree
to end one's inner struggle
is a salvation —

oh, Melpomene, my Muse,
I hear your sad lyre tune

21.

this love can crown you
or enslave you to pain,
my dear —
do keep your senses alive
and don't stop loving me!

22.

nothing is the same:
since your last good-bye
my wings are broken —
my tears are sad pearls of love
that belong only to you

23.

I close my eyes
dreaming of a re-birth
from my sadness —
but how to escape this
painful inner chaos?

24.

solemn poetry —
are you my rescue boat
or my hollow hope?
though Muses vouch for your worth
how to master your beauty?

25.

dancing hearts
beating in cheerful sync
our two souls are —

we feel life rhythms as if one,
and death did not exist

(*Lidia Hristeva, UK*)

NADEEM ISHAQUE

1.

fire burns east and west
two decades since twin towers
burst in horrid flames —
remember all who suffered
so no one is lost in vain

2.

as I close my eyes
a poetic reverie
in twilight unfolds —
at the threshold of a dream
night is waiting to be born

3.

in dazzling parade
of slick appearances
one cannot behold —
only to discerning eyes
is essence ever disclosed

4.

words bear no meaning
for in our shared solitude
silence is our bond —
let's be lonesome together
without a whisper till dawn

5.

in mellow moonlight
as if in a reverie
time came to a stop —
with moon still and breeze silent
tranquil she lay in my arms

(A. Nadeem Ishaque, USA)

JOJI VARGHESE KUNCHERIA

1.

this pandemic shows
we don't control our lives and
we need each other:
this is not just a truth
but a great revelation!

2.

oh, uncertain times
of fear, desperation
and seclusion!
whom can we turn to for
solace? the heart should respond

3.

which one will you choose:
worldliness or righteousness?
the two arch-rivals —
they decide your destiny
and of others around you

4.

life is not easy:
be a man of character
even when in pain —
although in anguish, you will
overcome the suffering

5.

heaven or hell?
not difficult to choose but
to live decently:
one is for those who love God
the other for those who don't

6.

overwhelming
is the monsoon's strength as
it sweeps over us;
the tug of war continues
and the heat is unyielding

7.

here they are at last:
the cool breeze and sunny days
prelude to monsoon...
days to enjoy the tropics
to their fullest before floods!

8.

the monsoon winds
make the coconut palms swing
like pendulums —
those toddy tappers are
rocking like in a trapeze

9.

the snake boats racing
make waters turbulent and
riverbanks vibrant —
cheering crowds celebrate
by playing whistles, horns, drums

10.

homeward-bound
I run fast to outrace
the torrential rain —
above me a flock of birds
rushes in search of shelter

11.

Christmas season:
festive spirits fill the air
as well as hearts —
the vendors, with a sore throat
from the shouting, clog the streets

12.

skies darken eastward
as billows of devouring
clouds gather above

fearful stars implore the wind
to blow them far away

13.

ominous dark clouds
gather over my head
making the sky black —
devoured by such a monster
are now the stars that sparkled!

14.

backpacks full of dirt
we carry on our shoulders:
let's do the cleaning!
it's time.. it's time.. to repent:
what moment's better than now?

(Joji Varghese Kuncheria, India)

KONSTANTINOS LAGOS

like a hungry wolf
he is preying upon me
inside a mirror —

there is no worst enemy
than the one we hide inside

(*Konstantinos Lagos, Greece*)

ARON LELEI

1.

I loved her dress
purple with shades of pink
so enticing:
my eyes were all for her
with my heart beating wildly

2.

violence strikes!
hatred turns men into beasts:
where's humanity?
armed with all kinds of weapons
hords of killers fill the streets

3.

watching the stars
lined up in constellations
of precious stones…

the colors of the rainbow
dress the sky like sparkling gems

(*Aron Cheruiyot Lelei, Kenya*)

MJ LEMON

1.

a tiny droplet
in a thirsty barley field
both my hands reach out...
and now a river snakes by
where farms and tractors tremble

2.

I knew a hero —
met him when he fought fires
living to face death

he disappeared in New York:
flames devoured his brawn, his will

3.

ferns, lakes, the woods live...
I walk and talk among them
but they do not speak —

>how to thank them for their warmth?
>I am here for their kindness

4.

darkness always comes...

at times I have company
but they cannot see —

>it clears a space in my heart
>and I find myself alone

5.

just as hard as steel
completely unforgiving
my polished switchblades

    I check them and they are safe
    then I glide across the lake

(Mj Lemon, Canada)

GEETA RADHAKRISHNA MENON

1.

the strong east wind blows
racing like never before
with a profound goal:
    cleaning the polluted air
    and healing my mind as well

2.

oh truthful mirror:
deep eyes that reveal your heart,
I see –

riot of aspirations
or pure soul's jubilation?

3.

sunset — will the sun
drown in hell or will heaven
open up its gates?
my friend, it's time to reflect
on 'karma', the law of deeds

4.

at the train station
he struggles with his anguish,
the young soldier —

   answer the call of duty?
   be with a sick mother...?

5.

a chameleon —
its changing colours from grey
to green pink red...
    ah, volatile emotions
    of the human heart!

(*Geeta Radhakrishna Menon, India*)

VALSA GEORGE NEDUMTHALLIL

1.

when you smile at me
I watch the curve of your lips
as they part to speak —
then I heed the sad whispers
of a torn, grief stricken heart

2.

the waves garland these
regal rocks with white blossoms
of fluffy froth

    above faintly woven skies
    the moon — a mute witness

3.

the sun spits fire
leaving earth's gaping mouth
to crave for moisture
    parched hearts crave the balm of love
    that evaporates like steam

4.

from the limpid pools
of her eyes, sad streams run down
her cheeks —
quivering, shaking, breaking
every fibre of her heart

5.

my heart keeps burning
at the thought of a farewell:
we are just pilgrims —
meeting to part in this world
heading to an unknown spot

6.

I crave for friendship:
loneliness, like a raider
stomps into being —

in a dull, desolate world
where shall I find company?

7.

the sun has set:
now in deep grey gown, the day
quietly glides through stars —
    time keeps galloping ahead
    as a racing horse, tireless

8.

starry sky above...
the *night queen* perfumes the air
as your arms wrap me —

    your breath falls on my neck as
    wingless I float in the sky

9.

I fenced myself
with the barbed wire of silence:
now a prisoner...
    in my solitary cage
    I wait for redemption

10.

tossed back and forth
a wilted flower floats
in whirling currents —

life moves on rudderless
to be cast in unknown shores

11.

two birds nestled close
on the branch of a fir tree
in the thick forest —
within those shady depths
friendship thrives through all seasons

12.

in the cloudy sky
the waning moon hangs cheerless
as one waiting fall

    I pause below, awaiting
    my final departure from life

13.

days draped in dense fog
and ground sheathed in hard ice

winter is glum —

so is old age with its frailty:
the winter of man's life!

14.

from derelict weeds
fair blossoms shyly peek out:
it's amazing...
talents can sprout from dark coves
giving sweet surprise to all!

15.

stubbornly she moves
from the shelter of the tree
the divorced woman —
struck by the heat of the sun,
she feels scorched in loneliness

16.

as a caged bird freed
leaps wildly across the sky
longing for freedom...

    he broke loose the chains that bound
    and soared into dizzy heights!

17.

like flowers
faded, wilted and withered
my dreams were crushed...
    yet they return to fresh life
    to fly sky high once again

18.

cuckoo's melody:
across woods and meadows
it's wafting —

as the lilts caress my ears
I look for Keats' Nightingale

19.

on my desk stays
a statue neatly chiseled:
a marvel of art —
in God's benign hands
we are nothing short of that

20.

when light fades
stars glow brighter in the sky
and so does love:

it shines more luminous
in times of adversity

21.

I close my eyes
to fend off all sad scenes
but mind is ajar...
it lets biting ants of pain
crawl through the narrowest slits

22.

a searing gash
the world still lives through
9/11

    as phoenix proudly rises
    from ashes life resurrects

(Valsa George Nedumthallil, India)

MOHAMMED ASIM NEHAL

1.

now is the time
to merge in the ocean
of love...
and survive together
until we too fall, like leaves

2.

from dawn to dusk
under the bright sun or
in the shadows...

how do they change color,
the human emotions

3.

we see the others
like ever-changing images
in a mirror —
sometimes larger or smaller
yet they remain the same

4.

locked inside the house
how can I pass my days
without meeting you?

the east wind brought the virus
that curtailed our freedom

5.

life until death:
a spiritual journey
that ends with hope...

    when the boat departs the world
    after a long pilgrimage

6.

when you gaze at me
while I pluck these rosebuds
their thorns pierce my heart —
my body shimmers with shame
as lust takes over my love

7.

the sun shining
over the misty mountain
melts the haze...
your trembling lips open up
making our tender love grow

8.

under clear blue skies
this autumn flowering
colors my mind...

old memories of parties
enlivened by birdsong

9.

the deafening sound
of the plane that flies away
from the battlefield...
are the corpses left behind
medals won for victory?

(*Mohammed Asim Nehal, India*)

NAMITA RANI PANDA

1.

the motherhood milk
that God sprinkled lavishly
turned to white lilies:

    source of heavenly bliss and
    symbol of humility

2.

the princess in pink
cheerfully lures us and
teach us a lesson:
to win something beautiful
we have to face prickly thorns

3.

a bright star I am
that ever keeps on glowing
to see you shining —
but you can feel my presence
only when you're in darkness

(*Namita Rani Panda, India*)

ANNETTE POTGIETER

1.

the crystal vase with
sandblasted proteas lies
shattered as our dreams
does it matter still that we
never climbed the Cederberg?

The protea cryophila is a 'near threatened' (NT) shrub, confined to the Cederberg mountains (Western Cape, South Africa).

2.

you gasp and step
into the valley of death
daddy....
the crisp morning air blurs
my sight — hazy hills afar

3.

your silhouette fades
as you stroll into the mist —

who could make you stay?

the cliff swallows also
seek another summer

4.

as she ponders
on her sins she wonders

what colour is grace?

it's the colour of the winds
that swept up yesterday's dust

5.

throughout history
abhorrent deeds of mankind
are recorded

and brave sacrifices lie
buried with heroes — unsung

6.

down the river
all the words I spoke float

and you...

how weary you must be
to have missed the lifeline

7.

forgotten outside
the satin nightdress quivers
under silver skies

tracing the curves on my skin
my love, tune my sighs tonight

8.

beneath flaming hair
and freckles he's still a boy
at thirty-two

so many years since that crash...
more than all his frail fingers

9.

would the saws grow still
if trees had deep amber eyes
ruefully pleading?

woe to mankind — suffering
from selective blindness!

10.

soon the days shrunk
like woolen pullovers
in my tumble dryer...

a lone pair of socks left out
dry in the winter sun

11.

only dust remained
on the long since empty shelves
of the oak cupboard

once sweet smelling linen sheets
filled the old wood with summer...

12.

have you noticed
how the shadows on the wall
stretched, towards sunset?

even moonlight hours stretch
as I listen for a bird

13.

oh, to colour
those gray shaded days of life
with pastel crayons

bright yellow for happiness
but for nostalgia soft blue

14.

I catch your words
like butterflies in a net
then set them free

the flutter between blossoms
ah, those belong to the sky!

15.

oh to catch your thoughts
in a butterfly's net, and
keep them in a jar!

sweet and slightly bitter
like bottled marmelade

16.

let me linger here
inside your careful words
where I'm safe from harm

the howls of foraging dogs
drift across the barren planes

17.

the noon sky
hides a breathless beauty
in plain blue sight

it changes colour by night
to reveal sparkling stars

18.

a dry east wind blows
over blazing barchan dunes
in the Sahara —
so far away the coolness
of the cumin scented night

Author's note:
A barchan, or barkhan dune, is a crescent-shaped dune.

136

19.

"*goodbyes*"
smother "*hellos*"
at the station —

trains abuzz with passengers
arriving and departing

20.

gifts in bright paper
tied with red and golden bows
this festive eve

even the sky is wrapped
in crimson clouds tonight

21.

roasted chestnuts and
gingerbread with cinnamon —
warm scents of Christmas...

sweet as fresh hay and the breath
of a babe that silent night

22.

now memories fade
as footprints in light snow
on Christmas eve —

the flicker of candlelight
as we unwrap fragile hearts

23.

I pray for peace
and stars in all children's eyes
this Holy Night:
for dirty hands and tiny
toes tired of running from wars

24.

a cool stream's burble
or the crunch of shriveled leaves
are gentle sounds —

as is the purr of the pen
when your heart speaks tanka

25.

what then is real?
is it the sun on my skin
or your pale blue ink?

you write sweet words — and I
stir them into my coffee

26.

I close my eyes
and bury my nose
in freshly cut hay —

you fled our golden fields with
the scent of earth in your beard

27.

fingers tapped and slid
as her darting eyes were glued
to square sheets of glass —

where's the little girl who gazed
through those rainy windows, now?

28.

she begs for two lines
on the pregnancy test
after many tries —

elsewhere, in a rusty bin,
a newborn wrapped in paper

29.

rows of words
on the crisp pages of my
dictionary —

but no definitions
for this feeling in my chest

30.

an open wound
dressed with used bandage:

nostalgia —

how to separate this grief
from our blissful love back then?

31.

it hurts
when you throw words in the wind
then watch them rain —

I left my umbrella home
as you used to bring sunshine

32.

my brown irises
diluted with joy are now
hazel-brown...

as old wood bark in summer
or the birthmark on your chest

33.

how many prayers
have I whispered to heaven

did angels count?

as many as the feathers
of a thousand wings

34.

moonlight picnics
in a rocking vessel
on the blue Danube —

memories are a haven
from life's ruthless tidal waves

35.

my soul wears gear
and backpack for this steep
mountain ridge

from high alpine peaks I dream
of your endless green plateaus

36.

under Greek sunsets
we peeled and diced refreshing
summer salads

bright pink watermelon
with crumbly feta cheese

37.

soiled with mud and blood
the high noon sun scorched
the child soldier
his abandoned wire toy
in the shade of a tree fern

38.

unkindled passion
curled into a tender bud
between her thighs —

absurd the mutilation
before the first blossom bloomed

39.

on the outside
of cardboard covers
the balladeer's name —

his soul is inside... blue
as the pressed forget-me-not

40.

still a boy — his skin
the colour of farm land
rich in humus...

he sells ripe bananas
on the side of a dirt path

41.

his glass was filled
to the brim with pain
like bitter wine...

remembering sweet lips
on Tuscan's purple vineyards

42.

chained to a dead tree
she licks the dirt from her
breeder's hand —

that same hand holding the bills
with which her pup was bought

43.

when you spread your wings
and soared towards open skies,
you left one feather —

that's when we knew you were
a lone bird on a fishpond

44.

last prayers were choked
before iron wings crashed
on 9/11 —

sparrows flap above bowed heads
at the memorial site

45.

the scorching sun sinks
beyond parched mountain ridges
come soon thunder clouds!

how I long for autumn rains
to quench my burning thoughts

46.

strawberry picking
under twilight skies, I taste
heart-shaped memories...

even in the dark I blushed
that first time your lips found mine

47.

still a child, almost,
she sighs in white wedding dress...

bliss of innocence!

spring will not last a lifetime
neither will her sunny smiles

48.

pomegranate blossoms
caressed by golden sunrays —

petals turn to fruit...

sweet as Solomon's Songs
and your kisses on my breasts

49.

pink toes and first steps
delightful gurgling laughter

such a gorgeous babe!

you are the breath in my lungs
the crystal voice in my throat

50.

in a dewdrop drowns
the white and yellow daisy...

will the morning sun

wipe the tears of the night
from my summer lawn and face?

51.

with broken lips
I kissed a salt pillar
tasting the ocean

and all our happy summers
on black and white photographs

52.

imagination...

the cold skin of lonely nights
as winter winds wail

is it not your longing voice?
alas — a mere taunting thought

53.

the wind and I smell
the summer breath of cotton
as we dance outside —

a red ladybug alights
onto the laundry basket

54.

like a winter throw
pull me tight under your chin

it is cold outside

freshly fallen white crisp snow
covered yesterday's prints

55.

politicians
scatter solemn promises
like breadcrumbs —

soon birds swoop in to peck
idle words and voters' hopes

56.

tentacles searching
the snail glides at early dusk —

what's for dinner?

escargots de bourgogne
served warm on a sandstone plate

57.

does she bite her lip
when she is afraid or shy?

behind the cloth mask

her voice is tied to her tongue
and sandwiched to her face

58.

fists clench iron bars
in a place of vain regrets —

could the clock go back!

his arms would hold his sweet wife
in a modest but warm home

59.

a soulful tune drifts
from the violin of the
street musician — he
keeps copper coins in a mug
but gold in his fingertips

60.

intoxicated,
he slept under bridges with
foggy memories:

his mothers soft fingers
and warm croissants for breakfast...

61.

at the open grave
mourners wear grim faces as
an earthy scent drifts...

but not from curving wet fields
sprinkled with red poppies

62.

if you carved your words
in her skin and heard her scream
your tongue would pause

but in silent pain she wilts
in the prison of your voice

63.

can the love of friends
shield the heart from the brain?

major depression —

a lone, long dive uncaged
into a shiver of sharks

64.

delightful art!

a charcoal pencil face
full of wrinkles...

yet on skin we try so hard
to hide every spot and line

65.

after the first frost
all petals of the red rose
turned black as sorrow,

yet the petite snowdrop
still wears its pure white blooms

66.

how it strives to trace
the blurring birds' path aloft
from below —

the song sparrow
with clipped feathers

67.

birds sing in the rain
an ode to the earthworm
and all souls outside —

water trickles from wet strands
past the dimple in my neck

68.

by silver moonlight
you began your artwork
showcased by dawn:

a flock of flapping wild geese
on rose and blue dappled skies

69.

the moth orchid
pouts her lower lip, coyly
to charm butterflies —

flap-flap they glide, surrender
to pollinate her flower

70.

dry leaves and dust
twirl down the busy road...

oh August winds!

even my sorrows are blown
against somber concrete walls

71.

lying on the grass...
white balls of cotton drift
against smooth blue skies —

crickets chirp whilst beetles drone
and the mantis prays for rain

72.

dangling from a branch
red apples dot the sky:

a ripe temptation!

the worm gobbles a tunnel
through juicy ivory flesh

73.

butterflies on
pansy blooms and lavender
find their fleeting joy —

the shy luna moth reveals
its rarely glimpsed beauty

74.

even the trees gasp
in smog and sour rainfall...

where have those days gone?

when the twilight air was sweet
with night-blooming jasmine breath

75.

a breeze carries
the song of the wild river
through open curtains —

do you think of me too
as I watch the silent moon?

76.

in this cold weather
sips of creamy hot chocolate
warm my lips

almost like your lips did
when we kissed in summer rain

77.

meticulously
the cobweb-spider spins
a dense web…

who can untangle those
caught in the liars' lies?

78.

will anything change
should I allow this anger
to reach my tongue?

the same tongue that tested
frostings for our wedding cake…

79.

meeting an old friend
over mild floral tea
on the veranda...

cups with hand painted pansies
and begonias in pots

80.

all in a day:

morn arose fair skinned, clothed
in pearly dew drops;

evenfall salutes (blushing)
as the sun blinks good night

(*Annette Potgieter, South Africa*)

UDAYA R. TENNAKOON

1.

through the mind's eyes
I enter the deception
of the world;
but then the pulse of my heart
adds wisdom to the vision

2.

the fresco
I painted on the wall
stands silent:

it endures any absence
because truth is behind it

3.

nothingness
wherein everything repeats
itself,

as the broken promise
made by humans to themselves

(Udaya R. Tennakoon, Switzerland)

HANS VAN ROSTENBERGHE

1.

the river of love
flowing still out of my heart
sinks fast in the sand...
the stream fumbles and ends
before it can meet the sea

2.

a lovely fruit
    once a sakura blossom
    so much cherished...

out of my life is now
    completely out of reach

(*Hans Van Rostenberghe, Malaysia*)

STEVEN R. VOGEL

1.

march of purple blooms,
color evoked from brown grass,
seeped in lush silence —
not one throat to elocute
a wind so full of swallows

2.

summer runs green through
cupped hands drip orange over
and blanched feet perceive —
in prisming color
liveliness revanishes

3.

all so unlikely,
music, dance, and poetry
carve ornate arcades —
like or not we play at life
festival that it is

4.

one small day I came
to see the throngs of people
fit as kindness —
passing bright songs and kisses
among reddening faces

5.

while you slept I wept
the tears of ashes fallen
from gentle years —
I woke into your sleep
to soothe better memories

6.

light on the ground
lifts the spruce over snow,
round to its base —
a wordless hover drapes
the hole over pricked arms

Author's note:
"The snow that catches on the branches doesn't make it to the ground, so the tree appears to be standing in a hole. The 'hole' draped over arms suggests interment" (S.V.)

7.

wolves and watchdogs
cannot tell themselves apart,
fall's iniquity —
the plethora of quaint barks
at enmity come down

Author's note:
"Enmity of various kinds began with the Fall. I am at enmity with the Fall Season" (S.V.)

8.

few live large
deserts with completed seas,
sporting each stranger —
who will approach hopping
animals baffled for life?

Author's note:
"This one is a 'tease' on Australian life and culture" (S.V.)

9.

old to your wedding,
the wine in our cellar ripe,
portent and pine boards —
sewn logs born long before
you walked the thirsty desert

"For Ken and Lynn" (S.V.)

10.

the waned moon dawdles
among gelatinous stars,
shaven afterthought —
I hold your hand on cold grass
to decipher crooning dew

11.

slid down,
hurled from a comma
to alight—
backside or afoot,
played from the sky in giggles

Author's note:
"This one is a simple (child's) ride down the slide at the park" (S.V.)

12.

you climbed a fall sky,
perfect blue peace, your breath hope,
each rising step light—
returned through odious smoke,
a black halo on the dead

9/11 anniversary.

13. [*variation on n.12.*]

they climb the pure sky
breathing hope into blue peace,
each rising step light —
then they descend through foul smoke,
as black halo on us all

14.

I close my eyes
and the world becomes ether
diaphanous pain—
but love's hard eye must see
touchable shapes for kindness

15.

if I live I must
be for love as love is life,
and I would live —
moon tell me you aren't watching
kindness lack for giving

16.

I can't wait to see
what someone has been cooking
on the iron stove —
grandma used to stew okra
with tomatoes and bacon

(*Steven R. Vogel, USA*)

CAROLINE WATSHAM

1.

let the sun be stilled
suspended in frozen time
to be reborn
    the smallest candle flame
    enlightens me anew

2.

sweet snowdrops emerge
like milky droplets through frost
to nourish my soul
    my faltering infant steps
    tread lightly on the earth

3.

carpets of flowers
herald spring's arrival
as yet unshaded
    I walk the fragrant pathways
    towards my destiny

4.

the world erupts:
Pan paints the trees brazen green
as sap rises

    come join a ring with me, love
    'tis almost fairy time

5.

now the heat-blown days
seductive in their langour
shine at their most bright
    yet with the brightest light
    must fall the darkest shadows

6.

Earth gives up her gifts
as flowers give way to seeds:
treasures to be shared
    what is given now will be
    my comfort in leaner times

7.

summer's decline brings
the balance of night and day
so light and shade match
　　and still I walk the tightrope
　　spanning hope and despair

8.

the light has dwindled
and sweet darkness whispers
"your work is done"
　　as spirits sing through the veil
　　I'm ready to step across

(*Caroline Watsham, UK*)

SOMAYEH ZARE

1.

each friendship you make
in the garden of love is
a seed to be sown —
which one would resist frost
and would sprout despite the drought?

2.

every harsh moment
needs your lover's strong hug
as an act of love —
what a nightmare life can be
without the comfort of love!

3.

they seem thoughtful —
the whispers you hear from him
everywhere...
the devil cooks words as meals
but who can smell his poison?

4.

love can be lost
when the words of lovers
lose their fragrance —
how wonderful when lovers
proclaim love in scented words!

5.

I swear on the past —
I swear to the world that took
my wings and my dreams:

I'm going to break your rules —
I will be someone else's wings

6.

inside the mirror
we all are souls
with colorless blood

> outside the mirror, cursed
> we are by our arrogance

7.

thousands were killed
by men consumed by hatred
who hijacked four planes —
with victims whispering
endless love to their dear ones

9/11 Anniversary

8.

sadly, too many
glossy magazine covers
kill women's soul —

girls enticed to look sexy:
thin waist, high heels, big butt... sham!

9.

somebody help me!
a girl in tears asks for help
but nobody cares —
    male chauvinism is widespread,
    in Belém as in Kabul

Editor's note:
Male chauvinism is the belief that men are superior to women.
"*in Belém as in Kabul*" — that is, "from Brazil to Afghanistan" — namely, all over the world.

10.

earth burns with fever
as soldiers instill poisons!
oh, men's bloody play...
    the devil rules the damn game
    by corrupting the whole world

(*Somayeh Zare, Iran*)

* * * * *

at the train station

my wife came with our daughter

on her back

I caught sight of her eyebrows

through a blanket of snow

Ishikawa Takuboku (1886–1912)
(translated by Roger Pulvers)

TANKA BY THEME

TANKA SEQUENCES

Here I propose a few tanka sequences, using 53 of the Authors' tanka. Obviously it is only a reading proposal: quite different sequences can be formed with the tanka submitted by the Authors.

I have collected the sequences according to 4 major themes:

NATURE

LOVE

FANTASY & DREAMS

THE WORST OF HUMAN NATURE

Tanka Sequence – Nature

A sequence of 12 Tanka

the waves garland these
regal rocks with white blossoms
of fluffy froth

    above faintly woven skies
    the moon — a mute witness

(*Valsa George Nedumthallil*)

~*~

with fluid movements
she performs her ballet
in the fairy blue:
white-dark wings sway back and forth
in flight — ah, the humpback whale!

(*Fabrizio Frosini*)

butterflies on
pansy blooms and lavender
find their fleeting joy —

the shy luna moth reveals
its rarely glimpsed beauty

(*Annette Potgieter*)

~*~

march of purple blooms,
color evoked from brown grass,
seeped in lush silence —
not one throat to elocute
a wind so full of swallows

(*Steven R. Vogel*)

cuckoo's melody:
across woods and meadows
it's wafting —

as the lilts caress my ears
I look for Keats' Nightingale

(*Valsa George Nedumthallil*)

~*~

a crescent rainbow
colours the summer sky
after the rainfall —
my weary heart leaps in joy:
a silent gleeful feeling

(*Lidia Hristeva*)

here they are at last:
the cool breeze and sunny days
prelude to monsoon...
days to enjoy the tropics
to their fullest before floods!

(*Joji Varghese Kuncheria*)

~*~

behind the girls' halls
the forest sublime sprawls large
under the sun —

banana leaves shade us
as we pick up kola-nuts

(*Birgitta Abimbola Heikka*)

a dry east wind blows
over blazing barchan dunes
in the Sahara —
so far away the coolness
of the cumin scented night

(*Annette Potgieter*)

~*~

a tiny droplet
in a thirsty barley field
both my hands reach out...
and now a river snakes by
where farms and tractors tremble

(*Mj Lemon*)

in Glasgow puppets
pulled by tarry threads spoke of
solemn commitments...
how to save the world from those
who just want to exploit it?

(*Fabrizio Frosini*)

~*~

another green world
and another yellow sun...

      carbon based life forms!

disposable and dead
as alkaline batteries

(*Carlo C. Gomez*)

* * * * *

Tanka Sequence – Love

A sequence of 12 Tanka

in mellow moonlight
as if in a reverie
time came to a stop —
with moon still and breeze silent
tranquil she lay in my arms

(*A. Nadeem Ishaque*)

~*~

strawberry picking
under twilight skies, I taste
heart-shaped memories...

even in the dark I blushed
that first time your lips found mine

(*Annette Potgieter*)

I loved her dress
purple with shades of pink
so enticing:
my eyes were all for her
with my heart beating wildly

(*Aron Cheruiyot Lelei*)

~*~

the fragrance of spring
is your velvety lips
kissing a blossom...
my first kiss is still with me
though I forgot how to kiss

(*Lidia Hristeva*)

the world erupts:
Pan paints the trees brazen green
as sap rises

    come join a ring with me, love
    'tis almost fairy time

(*Caroline Watsham*)

~*~

the sun shining
over the misty mountain
melts the haze...
your trembling lips open up
making our tender love grow

(*Mohammed Asim Nehal*)

starry sky above...
the *night queen* perfumes the air
as your arms wrap me —

    your breath falls on my neck as
    wingless I float in the sky

(*Valsa George Nedumthallil*)

~*~

the flight of a kite
taken by the reckless wind
lost in distant clouds

    and here the fall of her hair
    tethers my mind to the sky

(*Carlo C. Gomez*)

forgotten outside
the satin nightdress quivers
under silver skies

tracing the curves on my skin
my love, tune my sighs tonight

(*Annette Potgieter*)

~*~

your hair's on my face
and your light breath's a sweet breeze
on my neck...

    quietly we fell asleep
       each of us in our own dreams

(*Fabrizio Frosini*)

in this cold weather
sips of creamy hot chocolate
warm my lips

almost like your lips did
when we kissed in summer rain

(*Annette Potgieter*)

~*~

a bright star I am
that ever keeps on glowing
to see you shining —
but you can feel my presence
only when you're in darkness

(*Namita Rani Panda*)

* * * * *

Tanka Sequence – Fantasy & Dreams

A sequence of 18 Tanka

as I close my eyes
a poetic reverie
in twilight unfolds —
at the threshold of a dream
night is waiting to be born

(*A. Nadeem Ishaque*)

~*~

far out the window
I peer at the darkness still
what's there or who's there?

darkness paves the way for light
and I discern an image

(*Simon J. Daniel*)

imagination...

the cold skin of lonely nights
as winter winds wail

is it not your longing voice?
alas — a mere taunting thought

(*Annette Potgieter*)

~*~

the city lights shine
they shine soft as church candles
religiously so

    in the glow we know so well
    we reach for eternity

(*Carlo C. Gomez*)

was it worth the wait?

my unrequited love asks
on my grave...

when will I be given
a night free from such dumb dreams?

(*Fabrizio Frosini*)

~*~

death, my constant friend,
you have patiently called me
across life's wide stream —
the inexplicable dream
from which we yearn to awake

(*Nicholas Gill*)

beyond the edge
the deepest mystery looms:

end of the voyage?

but the cosmos of the mind
has no edges — no limits.

(*Fabrizio Frosini*)

~*~

through the mind's eyes
I enter the deception
of the world;
but then the pulse of my heart
adds wisdom to the vision

(*Udaya R. Tennakoon*)

deceptively
inside the cage of life
we're shown an exit —

    across turbulent waters
    our imagination swims

(*Fabrizio Frosini*)

~*~

I swear on the past —
I swear to the world that took
my wings and my dreams:

I'm going to break your rules —
I will be someone else's wings

(*Somayeh Zare*)

the river of love
flowing still out of my heart
sinks fast in the sand...
the stream fumbles and ends
before it can meet the sea

(*Hans Van Rostenberghe*)

~*~

a world of lilies
under an old wooden bridge
floats etched in her soul —
an imaginary world
but it lives on her palette

(*Sheryl Deane*)

the crystal vase with
sandblasted proteas lies
shattered as our dreams

does it matter still that we
never climbed the Cederberg?

(*Annette Potgieter*)

~*~

a chameleon —
its changing colours from grey
to green pink red...
    ah, volatile emotions
    of the human heart!

(*Geeta Radhakrishna Menon*)

while you slept I wept
the tears of ashes fallen
from gentle years —
I woke into your sleep
to soothe better memories

(*Steven R. Vogel*)

~*~

the light has dwindled
and sweet darkness whispers
"your work is done"
    as spirits sing through the veil
    I'm ready to step across

(*Caroline Watsham*)

inside the mirror
we all are souls
with colorless blood

    outside the mirror, cursed
    we are by our arrogance

(*Somayeh Zare*)

~*~

like a hungry wolf
he is preying upon me
inside a mirror —

there is no worst enemy
than the one we hide inside

(*Konstantinos Lagos*)

Tanka Sequence – The Worst Of Human Nature

A sequence of 11 Tanka

with tanks and missiles
the macabre dance starts and
evil rejoices —

he plays the role of a god
as mad as the worst devil

(*Fabrizio Frosini*)

~*~

the deafening sound
of the plane that flies away
from the battlefield...
are the corpses left behind
medals won for victory?

(*Mohammed Asim Nehal*)

engulfed in terror
lives were interrupted and
dreams left in rubble

    in the valley of despair
    memory and grief remains

(*Anna Banasiak*)

~*~

twenty years have passed
but the sorrow doesn't end
for those who bear it...
in a world so divided
their names are spoken once more

(*Fabrizio Frosini*)

throughout history
abhorrent deeds of mankind
are recorded

and brave sacrifices lie
buried with heroes — unsung

(*Annette Potgieter*)

~*~

beyond their pretense
what matters are the facts
seen by all —

and yet those who seek power
at all costs stop at nothing!

(*Fabrizio Frosini*)

covetousness —
a devil passed me by
and I knew evil…

he tore off the ear lobes
of a girl with gold earrings

(*Birgitta Abimbola Heikka*)

~*~

she begs for two lines
on the pregnancy test
after many tries —

elsewhere, in a rusty bin,
a newborn wrapped in paper

(*Annette Potgieter*)

somebody help me!
a girl in tears asks for help
but nobody cares —
    male chauvinism is widespread,
    in Belém as in Kabul

(*Somayeh Zare*)

~*~

they climb the pure sky
breathing hope into blue peace,
each rising step light —
then they descend through foul smoke,
as black halo on us all

(*Steven R. Vogel*)

now is the time
to change this harsh world into
a loving one
or the world will change your soul
into a wandering wolf

(*Lidia Hristeva*)

~*~

paulownia leaves...
impassable they've become,
you know —
no, there isn't anyone
I'm waiting for, be sure!

Imperial Princess Shokushi (or Shikishi) (1149?–1201)

ADDENDUM

About Tanka

Ancient Japanese Poetry

Glossary

Poet's biography

Poets Unite Worldwide

Other books Published

About Tanka

Fabrizio Frosini

A brief introduction to tanka poetry

Tanka poetry was born in Japan more than 1300 years ago, as a form of 'waka' —term meaning "*poetry in Japanese language*", to distinguish it from 'kanshi', that was poetry composed in Chinese by Japanese poets. The term waka originally comprised a number of different forms, most notably *tanka*, or "short poems", and *chōka*, "long poems". Tanka was the most widely-composed type of waka, made of five *ku* —phrase(s)— of 5–7–5–7–7 *on* (sound units); while chōka encompassed a repetition of 5 and 7 *on* phrases, with the last *ku* containing 7 *on*.

Although in the Nara period (710–794) and in the very first part of the early Heian period (794–1185), the court favored Chinese-style poetry (*the oldest collection of kanshi, the 'Kaifūsō', "Fond Recollections of Poetry", is dated 751; while the 'Man'yōshū', "Collection of Ten Thousand Leaves" —the oldest existing collection of Japanese poetry, compiled sometime after the year 759— contains 4,207 tanka, 265 chōka, but only 4 kanshi*), shortly afterwards waka poetry definitely superseded kanshi, so much so that Emperor Daigo ordered that the waka of ancient poets and their contemporaries were collected in the first imperial waka anthology (the *'Kokin Wakashū'* —"Collection of Ancient and Modern Japanese Poems"— usually abbreviated in 'Kokinshū', AD 905). Since only two forms of waka were in use at that time, tanka and chōka —but with the second hugely diminished in prominence—, the term waka became synonymous with tanka, and this word fell into disuse until Masaoka Shiki, at the end of the 19th century, revived it (along with the haiku form).

'Utakotoba', the standard poetic diction established in the Kokinshū, was considered as the very essence of creating a perfect waka, through a sound unit counts of 31 *on*, following the pattern 5–7–5 plus 7–7. Although tanka has evolved over the centuries, its ancient form hasn't changed.

The waka/tanka poetry has been particularly used for poems between lovers and in diaries; more generally, exchanging waka instead of letters in prose has been a widespread custom, since it is a lyric poem that, through its own flow and rhythm, can express the deepest feelings, emotions and thoughts —it is a kind of painting with words, that uses references to the natural world as well as to the inner feelings of our everyday life. Indeed, more generally, in Ancient Japan, especially among the educated citizens and members of the imperial court, Tanka was used as a scale to measure one's education, spiritual development, degree of culture, sensitivity to feelings and nature.

From waka, over time, a number of poetry genres developed, such as 'renga' (collaborative linked verse). As momentum and popular interest shifted to the renga form —in the Muromachi period (1336–1573)— waka was left to the Imperial court, and all commoners were excluded from the highest levels of waka training. Then, during the Edo period (1603–1868), renga poets were able to express broader humor and wit, through a simplified form of renga, where the use of commonly spoken words was allowed: the new style was called 'haikai no renga'*, or just '*haikai*' (*comical linked verse, also called 'renku'). What was traditionally referred to as '*hokku*', later called haiku, is the opening stanza, 5–7–5 'on', of a renga/haikai —indeed, the first document to record the word '*haiku*' is thought to be Hattori Sadakiyo's 'Obaeshu', (1663): it was used as an abbreviated form of "*haikai-no-ku*" (a verse of haikai).

In the second half of 1600, Matsuo Bashō (1644–1694), firmly committed to the cause of making haikai the equal of waka and renga, elevated this genre and gave it a new popularity. While waka and renga had belonged to the aristocratic world of court poetry and samurai culture, haikai became the genre of choice for commoners. All of the best haikai masters, used mainly the genre to describe nature and human events directly related to it, and stressed on the great significance of the opening stanza —hokku—, to give poetic relevance to such versification.

Hokku, removed from the context of renga and haikai, eventually became the stand-alone 17 *on* (5–7–5) haiku poetry form; Masaoka Shiki (1867–1902), then gave the term 'haiku' a special role, so to make it a genre of modern literature in its own right.

~*~

Historically, there were three major values people sought to achieve in Japanese culture:

   — *shin* (truth),
   — *zen* (goodness),
   — *bi* (beauty).

They represented philosophical, ethical and aesthetic goals respectively.

Waka (tanka) sought beauty first, followed by truth and some element of goodness.

Among the many aesthetic principles (or aesthetic tools/styles) that have arisen over the centuries, the following are worthy of mention (but we need to keep in mind that through the different ages, changes in their meaning have taken place): *wabi-sabi* (beauty in simplicity), that combines the two different concepts of *wabi* (subdued, austere beauty) and *sabi* (patinated loneliness and desolation); *mono no aware* (the pathos of things); *yūgen* (mysterious profundity); *miyabi* (refinement, elegance); *shibui* (simplicity); *shiori* (delicacy, kindness); *ushin* (depth of feeling); *hosomi* (slenderness); *karumi* (lightness); *iki* (refined style); *kire* (cutting); *jo-ha-kyū* (modulation and movement); *ensō* (void and absolution).

Notably, tanka poetry needs to make good use of '**sabi**' (melancholic sense of beauty; of something that has aged well, or has acquired a patina that makes it beautiful: the beauty accompanying loneliness, solitude), '**yūgen**' (literally translated as "depth and mystery" or "mysterious depth": spiritual profundity, or profound grace), and '*ma*' (awareness of time and space; creative imagination).

~*~

Formally, tanka is a non-rhymed *nature/human nature* poem with a pattern of 5-7-5-7-7 *on*/syllables. Indeed, saying that it must have 31 syllables is not correct, since they may vary — the important point is to respect the tanka metric:

short / long / short / long / long

"*short*", being a line of 5 or fewer syllables;
"*long*", a line of 7 or fewer syllables, but usually longer than the 1st and 3rd line.

Anyway, a poem of 5-7-5-7-7 syllables is not a tanka per se — *just as a 5-7-5 syllable poem is not a haiku per se*. In fact, much more important than syllable count is what we may call the 'spirit' of tanka. Thus you might also consider the concept of "pathos of existence" (life is fleeting) with its sense of "gentle desolation", as a key poetic device in Japanese tanka (as in haiku). And you should keep in mind that the musicality of the poem is important — it can be helpful to consider that since the age of 'Classical Japan' (Nara and Heian Period) waka/tanka was at the center of court life, and imperial competitions were often held, with the best waka chanted in gatherings convened by the emperor. Since then, tanka (even more than haiku) has been at the heart of all traditional culture in Japan, so much so that at the ceremony of the Utakai Hajime — the Imperial New Year's Poetry Reading, held on 1st January at the Tokyo Imperial Palace — tanka written by members of the Japanese royal family are recited aloud or sung (tanka also means "*short song*"), together with other poems selected from the best submitted for the occasion.

Tanka can be seen as divided into 2 parts: *kami-no-ku* ('upper phrase/poem', that is the first 3 units of 5-7-5 syllables) and *shimo-no-ku* ('lower phrase/poem', that is the last 2 units of 7-7 syllables). Yet, we must always remember that it should not be composed as if it were a single sentence simply divided into two parts. Furthermore, like haiku, when we write tanka we need to keep the verse open and a little (*just a little!*) fragmented or incomplete to encourage the readers to finish the verse in their imagination.

Tanka usually shows an intimate communication and it employs a turn, a pivotal image, which marks the transition from the examination of an image to the examination of the personal response. This turn (from the upper to the lower poem) often signals a shift or expansion of subject matter — if it needs, with a change in time, a change in subject, a change in person, or in place. in order to show this facet of a relationship. Such communication should show an association, comparison or contrast between images/ideas, or –better– take an image (presented/introduced in the "upper poem") and associate, compare or contrast it with the emotional situation of the writer (in the "lower poem"). We must emphasize "images", because (as in any fine poetry) it is better to show rather than to tell.

In order to enhance the internal communication, when writing a tanka, one of its lines (usually the middle line) can be used as a pivot line: a phrase that refers to both the first two lines and the last two, so that (either way) they make sense grammatically.

Despite the fact that usually a tanka is divided into the upper half of 5-7-5 and the lower half of 7-7 syllables, the turn can take place on a different line, thus dividing the poem differently from upper/lower half division. Yet, less experienced poets should stick to standard practice.

The upper unit of 3 lines (*kami no ku*) is, basically, the origin of the hokku —Masaoka Shiki, at the end of the 19th century, after he started advocating haiku reform (1892), reformed tanka poetry and gave the name haiku to the ancient 'hokku'.

Tanka shares some of the concerns of haiku poetry (for example, it may contains a *kigo*, season-word); yet, while haiku is objective, tanka is subjective, emotional, lyrical.

Another point that is often forgotten: tanka (as haiku) have no rhyme and have no title: a title is used only for a 'sequence' made of a number of poems (tanka or haiku) —a sequence that leads the reader through a progression designed by the poet.

Ancient Japanese Poetry

Daniel J. Brick

An Appreciation of Japanese Poetry

Preface

June is fleeting but its poetry, the fulfillment of Spring, stays behind the rush of time, anchoring our memories of this liberating season. So brief, so memorable. Such is the transience of Time but the permanence of Poetry. These two realities, so different from each other they are often called opposites, still fit together neatly. Disparate things find they are not incompatible after all: so separate, so united. And the surprise we register when we embrace this truth is the threshold to delight. Things are just things in themselves, as a philosopher would put it; but they are also part of a harmony, a unity, a wholeness of being, as a poet would put it. Sometimes when we are in a poetic state, things gather before our expectant eyes, and we are calmed by this perception; other times something is missing that focuses the things roaming in our neighborhood, and we are left with the nagging notion we just missed perfection. So close, so far away. In either case, what are we left with? A lingering aroma, a sensation of being touched, a cluster of images. The components of poetry are ever present. How can we pull them into poetic form, or must we wait until they are ready? So imminent, so elusive.

I wrote that paragraph to illustrate a quality of Japanese poetry, perhaps the Japanese Aesthetic as a whole. But is this not the way we perceive and treasure the world around us? Is it not a universal perception of the whole of which we are conscious parts? We can explore this quality of Japanese poetry by referring to one of its major influences over the centuries, namely, Buddhism.

There is a concept called 'Co-dependent Origination'. Stated in philosophical language, it comes across as thoroughly abstract, removed from sensory experience, refined by discursive reasoning. However, it is actually a poetic apprehension of the unity of all things in existence. The Vietnamese Buddhist monk, Thich Nhat Hanh (born 1926), has illustrated Co-dependent Origination in a series of images and used no abstract words, not even the term itself. This is what he wrote, what we might well call a Prose Poem:

"If you are a poet, you will clearly see there is a cloud in this sheet of paper. Without a cloud there would be no water, without water the tree could not grow, and without trees there can be no paper. So the cloud is in here. The existence of the paper is dependent on the existence of the cloud. Paper and cloud are that close." [Excerpted from 'Being Peace', 1987]

Even the least poetically-inclined person has to assent to Thich Nhat Hanh's statement — Paper and cloud are that close. What this example reveals is that poetry concerns itself with relationships, between things, between people and things, between people. A philosopher would not necessarily illustrate this concept with things, that is images. He or she would say the concept means that nothing is isolated in its own existence, but is rather involved continually with other things in a series of relationships.

This line of reasoning brings us to a crucial difference between western and Japanese poetries. It is the issue of figurative language — metaphor, simile, personification, et alia — common to all poetry. However, the unique Japanese forms of the haiku and tanka do not rely on figurative language. In western poetry such techniques are essential and often the very source of poetic magic. And it is the Buddhist concept of Co-dependent Origination which functions in Japanese poetry instead of figurative language.

What techniques like metaphor and simile do is to highlight a resemblance between two disparate things. But the resemblance is quite limited. Just at random I picked a passage from the American poet Delmore Schwartz: *"We are Shakespeare, we are strangers."*

The two halves seem to be in opposition: the first phrase praises us as if we share an identity with the greatest poet of the English language, but the second half withdraws the hyperbole as if we have nothing so grand in common. But both halves express a limited truth: we are all like Shakespeare when we speak English, we are co-creators of that language as we use it. But We suggests familiarity in a community, and the connection to Shakespeare is just not firm enough to overcome those things that makes us just unmet shadows to others. As you can see the resemblance expressed in a metaphor is very limited. That's why western poets have fuss over them, multiply them, seek out the most striking parallels. But the concept of Co-dependent Origination does not depend on a poet's special insight or verbal cleverness. It is embedded in the Buddhist overview of nature linking all of us on the profoundest level of shared being. Thus, the poet Saigyō addressed another animal as 'Tomo' or companion. He did not need to seek out resemblances that would become the poem's figurative language. All around him the world of nature was already a unified realm of beings.

Saigyō Hōshi [born Satō Norikiyo, 1118–1190]

Saigyō's life spanned the entire 12th century, a time of decadence, savagery and civil war. His response was to oppose these evils in his personal life by embracing with complete commitment the Buddhist values which offered a Path beyond the suffering of a broken society. This commitment led him to reject courtly life and its privileges and become a monk, a hermit monk, given to wandering the countryside.

Buddhism certainly gave his life a firm discipline and its essential attribute of compassion filled his being with loving kindness toward fellow human beings. However, the native religion of Shinto with its reverence for nature was deeply embedded in his consciousness. Basho, who revered Saigyō, said he possessed "*a mind both obeying and at one with nature throughout the four seasons*". This is high praise, acknowledging Saigyō's moral development, and it highlights the source of his spiritual excellence.

Saigyō excelled in the Waka or Tanka form of verse, that is, a thirty-one syllable poem, fourteen syllables longer than the later Haiku form. Writing poetry was a requirement in courtly life, and there is a strong current of competiveness among the aristocrats competing with each other to gain the most prestige. Poetry may be the only possession of this life Saigyō took with him, and his life as a monk purged his poetry of any traces of that venal pursuit of social advancement. Saigyō voluntarily left this aristocratic life of privilege and pleasure and chose a life diametrically opposite in values and habits. He also chose to be a Pilgrim Monk, wandering the country-side with no monastery to call home. He also assumed the identity of a Hermit, living alone in the splendid solitude of the mountains.

Was it easy for Saigyō to live alone and apart from others? His poems tell us he struggled mightily to fulfill his vows. He was not yet an enlightened being with a calm and focused mind, but a human being still, assailed by passions, longings and the very fact of desire in which the Buddha has located the source of our unhappiness. Consider these tanka:

1.
All so vague:
in autumn the reasons why
all fall away
and there's just this
inexplicable sadness.

2.
Journeying alone:
now my body knows this absence
even of its own heart,
which stayed behind that day when
it saw Yoshino's treetops.

These poems confess a crisis of loneliness, a time of inner unrest and outer confusion. The solitude he embraces is causing acute pain:

3.
Thought I was free

of passions, so this melancholy
come as surprise:
a woodcock shoots up from marsh
where autumn's twilight falls.

4.
I'll never forget
her look when I said goodbye..
especially since,
as keepsake she set her sorrow–
filled face on the moon above.

5
Long-living pine,
of you I ask: everlasting
mourning for me and
cover my corpse; here is no
human to think of me when gone.

Saigyō is so completely honest to himself in these poems. There is no pretence or vanity in his self-image: he admits the failure of his spiritual quest but does not surrender to sense of failure. He persists in Buddhist practices. The contemporary American Buddhist poet, Gary Snyder, clarified this endeavor: "*The full moon has long been a Buddhist symbol of the Tathagata or perfect and complete Enlightenment*". And Saigyō devoted himself to what Gary Snyder called, "*the long and steady contemplation of the moon*", preparing his mind for the flood of Enlightenment.

6.
We would together
make the journey, I on land
and it in the sky,
if the moon comes out to stay:
empathy both ways.

7.

It will be good:
my body may cry itself into
a pond of tears,
but in it my unchanged heart
will give lodging to the moon.

8.
Winter has withered
everything in this mountain place:
dignity is in
its desolation now, and beauty
in the cold clarity of its moon.

Eventually Saigyō achieved something of that cold clarity he observed in the moon. He was able to live a fully realized human life, reconciling dignity and desolation with Buddhist impartiality. His heart is still, his mind is focused: he has attained the spiritual condition which John Milton described at the end of his final poem, 'Samson Agonistes': "*With peace and consolation.. / And calm of mind, all passion spent.*":

9.
Limitations gone:
since my mind fixed on the moon,
clarity and serenity
make something for which
there's no end in sight.

10.
The mind for truth
begins, like a stream, shallow
at first, but then
adds more and more depth
while gaining greater clarity.

A poet from Nepal once differentiated Christianity and Buddhism: A Christian after death confronts judgment and either reward

253

or punishment will result. A Buddhist enters a realm of freedom, no confrontation stalling his liberation. In several of his poems written after he achieved an Enlightened Mind, Saigyō suggests he has already entered that realm of freedom while still inhabiting the sensory world as a flesh and blood creature. These poems are very restrained, they seem to come out a great stillness and only briefly linger in our world before they return to the stillness. Even falling blossoms in autumn or winter rain cannot disturb his poise and calm. And in spring he simply rejoices:

11.

A man whose mind is
at one with the sky-void steps
inside a spring mist
and thinks to himself he might
in fact step right out of the world.

Ono no Komachi [c. 825—c. 900]

In 905, the first imperial anthology of Japanese poetry, the Kokinshu, was compiled by the poet and scholar, Ki no Tsurayuki (872–945), who also wrote a luminous preface to the collection. It reads in part:

"Japanese poetry has its seeds in the human heart, and takes form in the countless leaves that are its words. So much happens to us while we live in this world that we must voice the thoughts that are in our hearts, conveying them through the things we see and the things we hear. We hear the bush warbler singing in the flowers or the voice of the frogs that live in the water and know that among all living creatures there is not one that does not have its song. It is poetry that, without exerting force, can move heaven and earth, wake the feelings of unseen gods and spirits, soften the relations between man and woman, and soothe the heart of the fierce warrior."

What an amazing statement! What Ki no Tsurayuki wrote encourages poets to cultivate a sensibility in sympathy with what he identifies as the essence of Japanese poetry, and he suggests a range of topics that will make their subject matter varied and surprising. He was clearly reflecting on what he saw in the current poetry scene, but his visionary statement also provides scope for poets in the long ages ahead. Tsurayuki's critical sense was very keen, and he included eighteen poems by the female poet, Ono no Komachi, who effortlessly embodies the special qualities of Japanese poetry his preface highlights.

His locating the origin of poetry in the human heart is especially true of Komachi's poems. One of her translators, Kenneth Rexroth, called his collection of her tanka, 'The Burning Heart'. Here is one of her tanka that illustrate that title:

1.
No way to meet him,
no moon to light his way,
I wake up with longing,
my chest a raging fire,
my heart in flames.

We don't know why her lover does not come. Perhaps the night is too dark and he fears for his safety, or perhaps he is a faithless lover. What we do know with unambiguous certainty is her erotic desperation. The imagery of fire to show her soul-state almost breaks the bounds of the carefully crafted tanka. But it doesn't. The poem is a perfect form enclosing fierce emotions.

Here is two other poems which originate in Komachi's troubled heart:

2.
Since my heart placed me
on board your drifting ship,
not one day has passed
that I haven't been drenched
in cold waves.

3.
I thought to pick
the flower of forgetting
for myself,
but I found it
already growing in my heart.

These two poems are written at a much lower level of emotional display, they are almost poems of quietude that recollect passion in moments of tranquility. Although the sheer emotional outburst of the first tanka is absent from these two, they both reveal her surrendering to an uncertain erotic destiny without hesitation.

Tsurayuki writes that poets convey their emotions indirectly, "*through the things we see and the things we hear*". Here are two beautiful examples of this poetic technique:

4.
O spider lily
that grows on the mountain
called Waiting,
is there someone you also
promised to meet this autumn?

5.
Seeing the moonlight
spilling down
through these trees
my heart fills to the brim
with autumn.

Tsurayuki affirms that "*among all living creatures there is not one that does not have its song*". This awareness not only shows respect for other creatures, it links us humans to them in a nexus of expression and communication. The native Shinto religion is imbued with this appreciation of all living things, and later Buddhist teachings would argue all things have Buddha-nature. This is analogous to a European Romantic poet declaring animals have souls and the natural environment is a spiritual presence. Consider these two tanka:

6.
This pine tree by the rock
must have its memories too:
after a thousand years,
see how its branches
lean towards the ground.

7.
The hunting lanterns
on Mount Ogura have gone,
the deer are calling for their mates..
how easily I might sleep.
if only I did not share their fears.

Tsurayuki's preface closes with four powers of poetry to accomplish amazing feats "*without exerting force.*" That provision that poetry does not exert force is especially pleasing considering the violent course of history in Japan and indeed elsewhere. Ono no Komachi lived in a society in which women were severely restricted in their behavior, so force was simply not available to her. And her poems reveal this in her passivity in the long run of her inner life as well as her outer life. Here are examples of that passivity, that surrendering to her erotic fate:

8.
The flowers withered,
their colors faded away,
while meaninglessly
I spend my days in brooding
and the long rains are falling.

9.
In the daytime
I can cope with them,

but when I see those jealous eyes
even in dreams,
it is more than I can bear.

10.
Without changing color
in the emptiness
of this world of ours,
the heart of man
fades like a flower.

Tsurayuki identifies two powers of poetry I do not find in Komachi's extant poems. Both relate to the higher realm of the gods and goddesses, and again I do not find this subject matter in her poems. He cites poems 'Moving heaven and earth' and 'Waking the feelings of unseen gods and spirits'. In fact, Komachi expresses a view that seems to be nihilistic:

11.
Sad –
the end that waits me –
to think at last
I'll be a mere haze
pale green over the fields.

Far from suggesting some unique impact on the powers of fate, this tanka suggests a gorgeous nothingness will follow mortal existence. She has no firm belief concerning our ultimate fate:

12.
This body
grown fragile, floating,
a reed cut from its roots..
if a stream would ask me
to follow, I'd go, I think.

But I do not want to close this commentary on Ono no Komachi on such a dour note. It is certainly accurate to say her poems that have survived are music in the minor key, that the frequent failure of her romantic gambits made her lament her fate, and that she had probably a melancholy disposition throughout her life.

But we must remember Ono no Komachi was fiercely committed to erotic desire and its fulfillment, and she was willing to suffer disappointment as she sought fulfillment in a lasting love that was not be her fate. And she poured that frustrated desire into her poetry, whose surface meaning details much heart-felt sorrow but whose inner meaning is a triumphant celebration of heart-felt ecstasy.

About 5 centuries after her death, the NOH master, Zeami Motokiyo (c. 1363–c. 1443), wrote a play about Ono no Komachi, 'Komachi At Sekidera'. At the end, as the spirit of Komachi performs a dance of reconciliation to her fate and earthly suffering, the Chorus celebrates the eternal value of the poetry that flowered from her tragic, joyous existence:

> *The words of poetry will never fail.*
> *They are enduring as evergreen boughs of pine.*
> *Continuous as the trailing branches of willow.*
> *For poetry, whose source and seed is found*
> *In the human heart, is everlasting.*
> *Though ages pass and all things vanish,*
> *Poems will leave their marks behind,*
> *And the traces of poetry will never disappear.*

(from the Anthology, 'Moments of Lightness', 2017)

Useful Glossary

Alphabet, Japanese: see Japanese Alphabet.

Anthologies of Japanese poetry: see Imperial Anthologies.

Asuka period: (538–710) the country evolved from the old Yamato adminis-tration to an Imperial system based in Asuka region, and the Yamato language became the common spoken language. Introduction of Buddhism in Japan hap-pened in this period. Some historians consider the Asuka period as part of 'Classical Japan', together with the Nara and Heian periods.

Azuchi-Momoyama period: also known as the late Warring Kingdoms period (1569–1603).

Bakufu: the military government of the shōgun, namely the shogunate.

Bunraku: a form of traditional Japanese puppet theatre.

Bashō Matsuo: (Ueno,1644–Ōsaka,1694) the greatest haikai master. He is quoted as saying, "Many of my followers can write hokku as well as I can. Where I show who I really am is in linking haikai verses." (Chris Drake, Journal of Renga & Renku, 2, 2012).

Bashō School: among the best Bashō's disciples, were Yamaguchi Sodo (1642-1716), Hattori Ransetsu (1654–1707), Mukai Kyorai (1651–1704), Nozawa Bonchō (1640–1714), and Hattori Toho (1657–1730).

Bashō Shichibu Shū: (or "Haikai shikibu shū") the Haikai Seven Anthologies of Bashō School, written by Bashō and eleven of his disciples. Some of the disciples edited the books under Bashō's direction.

Buson Yosa: one of the four great haikai masters (1716–1784).

Chadō: see 'Sadō' –the Japanese tea ceremony, also called *chanoyu*.

Chiyo-ni Fukuda: haikai poetess (1703–1775).

Chōka: "long poem", as opposed to tanka ("short poem"); see Waka.

Chōnin: "townsman/townspeople"; basically the equivalent of the European bourgeoisie –merchants and craftsmen, but also government officials of the lower rank–, social class born in the Edo period (1603–1868).

Daimyō: feudal lords.

Edo period: (1603–1868) or Tokugawa era, after the family who expressed the shōgun that time. After the "feudal" period (or medieval Japan, 1185–1573), the power once again became centralized in the hands of a hereditary shogunate. This happened when Tokugawa Ieyasu seized power and established a government based in Edo (Tokyo), while the emperor continued to reside in Kyoto. The shōgun subordinated the nobility, took control of religion, suppressed the protests and, by establishing uniform tax systems, bureaucracy and public spending, adjusted the whole economy (at least in the first part of the period). All this led to profound changes in Japanese society.

Ensō: void and absolution – aesthetic principle/style.

Fūga: high art (for Bashō, it was haikai itself).

Fūga-no-makoto: poetic truth or honesty (what Bashō called haikai truths).

Fueki: eternal essence; permanent values; tradition.

Fueki ryūkō: ("the unchanging and the ever changing") intended as a sort of positive balance between tradition and innovation.

Fujiwara no Kintō (966–1041): among other works, he wrote a waka collection called *Shuisho* (compiled 996–999), which became part of the third imperial anthology of waka from Heian period, the *Shūi Wakashū*. He also established the grouping of "Thirty-Six Poetic Geniuses" or Immortals (*Sanjūrokkasen*).

Fujiwara no Teika (1162–1241, late Heian/early Kamakura periods): Fujiwara Sadaie, called Teika, was one of the greatest Japanese waka poets and Japan's most influential poetic theorist and critic, whose critical ideas on composing poetry were studied until as late as the Meiji era (which began in 1868). Retired emperor Go-Toba (1180–1239) appointed him one of the compilers of the 8th Imperial anthology *Shin kokinshū* (c. 1205). In 1232 Teika was then appointed, by a different emperor, sole compiler of the 9th anthology, *Shin chokusenshū*, thereby becoming the first person ever to participate in the compilation of two such anthologies.

Furyu: special taste of artistic and poetic nature (a person with 'furyu' is a person who loves the arts, particularly poetry, and shows detachment from the mundane affairs).

Gendai haiku: modern/contemporary haiku; elements of gendai haiku are: free-form and experimental aesthetics, modernism, surrealism, social conscience, and so on —but even so, gendai haiku does not negate haiku tradition.

Genji Monogatari: "The Tale of Genji", written by Murasaki Shikibu at the beginning of 1000 (Heian period); considered as the first modern novel, it contains about 950 waka.

Hai: sense of humor.

Haibun: concise prose poem in haikai style, combining prose and haiku. The range of haibun is broad and frequently includes autobiography, diary, essay, prose poem, short story and travel journal. The term "haibun" was first used by Matsuo Bashō, in a letter to his disciple Kyorai in 1690.

Haiga: a style of Japanese painting that incorporates the aesthetics of haikai, and is accompanied by haiku. Yosa Buson painted many haiga with their own hokku (haiku).

Haijin: haiku writer/poet.

Haikai no renga (or comic renga): see haikai.

Haikai: short for *'haikai no renga'*, comic linked verse in playful character. At the beginning, haikai was lower in status to waka and renga, considered elite genres; this changed with Bashō. In the 17th century (Edo period), haikai no renga became the genre of choice for commoners. Haikai encompasses other poetic forms that embrace the haikai aesthetic, including haiku, senryū, haiga (painting and haiku), haibun (prose and haiku). The linked verse, renku, rose to a new popularity in Japan in the second half of the 20th century. Haikai does not include orthodox renga (*ushin* r.) or waka (tanka).

Haiku: the shortest form of Japanese poetry, as it is only 17 sound unit (*on*) long, with a 5-7-5 rhythm. It uses seasonal references (*kigo*, season words; *kidai*, season themes), *kire* (cutting), and aesthetic tools/styles to give the reader an instant sense of common experience and perception of the poet's feelings. Through cutting and juxtaposition, the poet can single out and emphasize a part of the haiku, thus creating a dramatic effect. The origin of haiku is the opening stanza (*hokku*) of haikai —indeed, the term haiku is the contracted form "*haikai no ku*" ("verse of haikai"), with the first recorded document dated 1663. At the end of 19th century, Masaoka Shiki used this term in place of hokku.

Heian period: (794–1185) named after the capital city of Heian-kyō (the modern Kyōto), it is considered the peak of the Japanese imperial court and noted for its art, especially poetry and literature.

Hiragana: form of kana (syllabic writing) used in Japanese, especially used for function words and inflections (see Japanese alphabet).

Hokku: the opening stanza in haikai-no-renga poetry.

Honkadori: allusion, within a poem, to an older poem, which would be generally recognized by its potential readers. Honkadori possesses the aesthetic qualities of yūgen and ushin.

Hosomi: slenderness.

Iki: refined style.

Imperial Anthologies (most significant): *Man'yōshū* ("Collection of Ten Thousand Leaves"), compiled c. 760 AD (Nara period), is the oldest poetic anthology of waka. *Kokin Wakashū*, or just Kokinshū ("Collection of Japanese Poems of Ancient and Modern Times"): first published c. 905, its finished form dates to c. 920 (Heian period). *Shin Kokin Wakashū*, or Shin Kokinshū ("New Collection of Ancient and Modern Poems") is the 8th poetic anthology, compiled 1205 (Kamakura period). Although, over the centuries, 21 anthologies of Japanese poetry were compiled at imperial request, the three named are the most influential poetic anthologies in Japanese literary history.

Issa Kobayashi: one of the four greatest haikai masters (1763–1828).

Izumi Shikibu (976?–1033?): considered by many as the greatest woman poet of the Heian period, she's listed among the 'Thirty-six Female Immortals of Poetry' (Nyōbō Sanjūrokkasen). She was contemporary of Murasaki Shikibu.

Japanese alphabet: the Japanese writing system originated through adoption and adaptation of the Chinese logograms, "hànzì". The Japanese language had no written form at the time Chinese characters were introduced. The Japanese term for the hànzì characters is *kanji*: it literally means "Han characters" (Chinese characters). Around 650 CE, a writing system called *man'yōgana* evolved that used a number of Chinese characters for their sound, rather than for their meaning: from it the modern kana syllabaries developed. Man'yōgana written in cursive style evolved into *hiragana*, a writing system that was accessible to women –who were denied higher education (Heian-era literature by women was usually written in hiragana). *Katakana* emerged from monastery students, who simplified man'yōgana to a single constituent element. Thus the two writing systems, hiragana and katakana (referred to collectively as *kana*), are descended from kanji. The two basic sets of characters, kana and kanji, are still used today. Kana characters are the closest thing to a western alphabet that exists in Japanese. Unlike letters in western alphabets, however, kana represent sounds (there are 46 Japanese kana/sounds), and not all western sounds are represented. The meanings and pronunciations of the two styles of kana –katakana and hiragana– are the same, though they are written in different styles. Hiragana characters are used for writing Japanese words, while katakana are used for western words imported into Japanese. Kanji characters are considerably more complicated: they are symbolic characters that represent specific words and concepts. Although the total number of kanji characters is disputed, they're said to be more than 50,000. The Japanese Ministry of Education compiled a list of 1,945 kanji characters, which are the most commonly used and considered the minimum number required for adult literacy; of them, 1,000 are the characters that Japanese children learn in elementary school.

Jo-ha-kyū: modulation and movement —aesthetic principle/style.

Juxtaposition: aesthetic style made possible by 'cutting' (*kire*); it contrasts two opposites together to unveil a surplus of words previously hidden, thus creating a dramatic effect.

Kabuki theatre: a classical Japanese dance-drama, sometimes called "the art of singing and dancing".

Kachōfūei: aesthetic principle ("the charm of nature as the heart of haiku") of the conservative haiku school directed by Kyoshi Takahama (1874–1959).

Kaifūsō: the oldest collection (compiled in 751) of Chinese poetry (*kanshi*) written by Japanese poets.

Kamakura period: (1185–1333) corresponds to the Kamakura shogunate, officially established in 1192 by the first shogun, Minamoto no Yoritomo, in Kamakura. It is known for the emergence of the samurai caste and for the establishment of feudalism in Japan.

Kana (characters): see Japanese alphabet.

Kanbun: ("Chinese writing") method of annotating Classical (Literary) Chinese so that it can be read in Japanese, used from the Heian period to the mid-20th century.

Kanji (characters): see Japanese alphabet.

Kanshi: "poems in Chinese", written by Japanese poets using *kanji* (Chinese logograms). It literally means "Han poetry". During the early Heian period, it was the most popular form of poetry among Japanese aristocrats. The earliest collection of kanshi was the *Kaifūsō*, one of the earliest works of Japanese literature (compiled in 751).

Karumi: lightness; "the poetic beauty reflected in its simplicity".

Katakana: form of *kana* (syllabic writing) primarily used for words of foreign origin (see Japanese alphabet).

Kake-kotoba: "pivot word"; a rhetorical device used in the Japanese poetic form waka (the earliest examples are from the Nara period). The presentation of multiple meanings inherent in a single word allows the poet a fuller range of artistic expression with an economical syllable-count —but kakekotoba translations can sometimes be meaningless by themselves, and need a context to bring out their meaning, since the kakekotoba can be translated with different meanings.

Kidai: seasonal theme(s).

Kigo: season word(s).

Kikan: seasonal feeling(s).

Kintsugi: the art of reassembling broken pottery (for the most precious items, even filling the lines of fracture with gold), in the suggestion that even the difficult memories are as valuable as the happiest.

Kire: cutting (through cutting and juxtaposition, the poet can single out and emphasize a part of his/her tanka or haiku).

Kireji: cutting word(s).

Kofun period: (250–538), named after the large tombs –kofun– built by the rulers. About 400 CE the country was united as 'Yamato Japan', with its political center in and around the province of Yamato (about today's Nara Prefecture).

Kokin Wakashū (or Kokinshū): see Imperial Anthologies.

Kokoro: feeling, heart, spirit.

Kokugaku (national learning): Edo era school of Japanese philology and philosophy, focussed in research into the early Japanese classics. extolled by Motoori Norinaga, it stated that the Japanese national character would reveal its splendor once the alien (Chinese) influences were removed.

Koto: the event, the process.

Ku: a stanza or a verse of haikai.

Ma: awareness of time and space; creative imagination.

Makoto: truthfulness.

Makura kotoba ("pillow words"): normal words used as codes to bring out a mood or mental scene for the reader (see also '*Utamakura*': "poem pillow").

Man'yōgana: ancient writing system that employs Chinese characters (*kanji*) to represent the Japanese language. It was the first known *kana* system (see Japanese Alphabet) to be developed as a means to represent the Japanese language phonetically. In use since at least the mid seventh century, it was named such after the *Man'yōshū*, since the anthology was written in man'yōgana.

Man'yōshū: see Imperial Anthologies.

Meiji period: or Meiji restoration (1868–1912) of imperial power; it represents the first half of the Empire of Japan during which Japanese society moved from being an isolated feudal society to its modern form. It was succeeded by the Taishō period.

Miyabi: refinement, elegance.

Mono: the thing.

Mono no aware: the pathos of things.

Motoori Norinaga (1730–1801): Japanese scholar of Japanese philology (Kokugaku school); he extolled *mono no aware*, as a particular Japanese sensibility that he claimed forms the essence of Japanese literature.

Mujō: impermanence.

Murasaki Shikibu (973?–1014?): the author of the 'Genji Monogatari' ("The Tale of Genji"), written at the beginning of 1000 (Heian period), which is considered the "first modern novel", and the first psychological novel.

Muromachi period: (1336–1573), also known as the Ashikaga shogunate. Officially established in 1338 by the first Muromachi shogun, Ashikaga Takauji —two years after the brief Kenmu Restoration (1333–36) of imperial rule was brought to a close—, it ended when the 15th and last Ashikaga shogun, Ashikaga Yoshiaki, was driven out of Kyoto by Oda Nobunaga.

Nara period: (710–794) while the Japanese Imperial House historically emerged in the sixth century AD, the first permanent capital, Heijo-kyo (modern Nara), was founded in 710, and soon became a center of art, religion (Buddhism) and culture. Nara, was modeled on the Chinese T'ang dynasty capital, Ch'ang-an. Chinese language and literature were studied intensively and the Chinese characters were adapted to the Japanese language. The *Kaifūsō*, collection of Chinese poems (*kanshi*) written by Japanese poets, and the *Manyō-shū*, anthology of *waka* poetry, were compiled this period.

Nō theater: (*nō*, meaning "talent/skill") traditional Japanese theatrical form and one of the oldest extant theatrical forms in the world —developed from ancient forms of dance drama and from various types of festival drama at shrines and temples, it became a distinctive form in the 14th century. Because of the high degree of stylization, performing noh is not like acting in realistic Western theatre: noh performers are more storytellers who use their visual appearances and their movements to suggest the essence of their tale rather than to enact it.

On: refers to counting phonetic sounds in haiku, tanka, and other forms of Japanese poetry.

Onitsura Uejima: haikai master (1661–1738) who belonged to the Danrin school, founded by Nishiyama Sōin (1605–1682).

Ono no Komachi (c. 825? – c. 900?): one of the *Rokkasen* —the six best waka poets of the early Heian period— and also one of the "Thirty-six Immortals of Poetry" (*Sanjūrokkasen*), she is one of the most frequently quoted poets of the *Kokin Wakashū*, the first Imperial anthology of waka. Komachi is, perhaps, the earliest and best example of a passionate woman poet in the Japanese canon and, together with Murasaki Shikibu and Izumi Shikibu, the most loved poetess in Japanese history.

Renga: genre of Japanese collaborative poetry in which two or more poets supplied alternating 'ku' (verse). It was one of the most important literary arts in pre-modern Japan. The form developed fully in the 15th century, when a distinction came to be drawn between *ushin renga* (orthodox renga), which followed the conventions of court poetry, and *mushin renga*, or haikai (comic renga). A famous renga master was the poet and Buddhist priest Sōgi (1421—1502). The *hokku* was originally the opening stanza, of 5–7–5 'on', of a renga. See also haikai.

Renku: linked stanzas (*haikai-no-renga* –see haikai). It has known a new popularity, in Japan, since the second half of the 20th century.

Rokkasen: the "six poetry immortals" —Ōtomo no Kuronushi, Ono no Komachi, Ariwara no Narihira, Kisen Hōshi, Sōjō Henjō, Fun'ya no Yasuhide— waka poets named by Ki no Tsurayuki in the introduction of the Anthology *Kokin Wakashū* (Kokinshū).

Ryūkō: fashion, newness, innovation and originality.

Sabi: patinated loneliness; melancholic sense of beauty.

Sadō: the Japanese tea ceremony (also called 'chanoyu' or 'chadō'); Zen Buddhism was a primary influence in its development. Although it is said that tea was introduced to Japan at the beginning of the 9th century by the Buddhist monk Eichū, on his return from China, it was around the end of the 12th century, that the style of tea preparation (called 'tencha' –in which powdered 'matcha', kind of green tea, was placed into a bowl, hot water added, and the tea and hot water whipped together) was introduced by the monk Eisai. Later, during the Muromachi period (1336–1573), the tea ceremony began to evolve its own aesthetic, in particular that of 'sabi' and 'wabi' principles. Rikyū (1522–1591), is considered the historical figure with the most profound influence on the "way of tea" [the principles he set forward —harmony (和 wa), respect (敬 kei), purity (清 sei), and tranquility (寂 jaku)— are still central to it].

Saigyō (Satō Norikiyo; 1118, Kyoto–1190, Ōsaka): born into an aristocratic military family, as a youth he worked as a guard to retired Emperor Toba, but at age 22 he quit worldly life to become an Amida Buddhist monk (Pure Land Buddhism). Saigyō's poetry focuses not just on 'mono no aware' (sorrow from change) but also on 'sabi' (loneliness) and 'kanashi' (sadness). He was a good friend of Fujiwara no Teika, and many of his waka are included in the imperial anthology *Shin Kokin Wakashū* (or Shin Kokinshū, 1205), while *Sankashū* ("Collection of a Mountain Home") is his best known personal waka collection. Matsuo Bashō was a great admirer of Saigyō.

Saijiki: extensive, prescriptive lists of kigo divided by season.

Sakoku: ("locked country") seclusion from the outside world —the Tokugawa policy of isolation that remained in effect until the arrival of the Black Ships of Commodore Matthew Perry, in 1853.

Sanjūrokkasen: the "Thirty-Six Immortals of Poetry", anthology compiled by Fujiwara no Kintō in the early 11th century.

Senryū: pen name of Karai Hachiemon (1718–1790); after his death, his pseudonym was adopted to identify a new genre of haikai.

Senryū: comic verse of 5–7–5 syllables, born from a form of witty and satirical linked verse centered on the human being, the maekuzuke. Senryū is a sharp-witted and somehow cynical insight into the world of human nature, so weak and imperfect, but also poignant. It can be said that, as a new haikai genre, senryū was born when the tsukeku which won the maekuzuke competition, "A Ten Thousand-Stanza Competition, Judged by Senryū", were published for the first time; it happened in 1760.

Shibui: simplicity.

Shiki Masaoka: pen-name of Masaoka Noboru (1867–1902), major figure in the development of modern haiku poetry.

Shin Kokin Wakashū (or Shin Kokinshū): see Imperial Anthologies.

Shiori: delicacy, kindness.

Shōgun: "commander-in-chief" or military ruler/dictator. During the period from 1185 to 1868 (with exceptions) the shoguns were the de facto rulers of Japan; although nominally they were appointed by the Emperor as a ceremonial formality. The shogun's officials were collectively named the 'bakufu', and were those who carried out the actual duties of administration, while the imperial court retained only nominal authority.

Shōwa period: (1926–1989) refers to the period of Japanese history corresponding to the reign of the Shōwa Emperor, Hirohito.

Shūi Wakashū ("Collection of Gleanings"): usually known as 'Shūishū', it is the 3rd imperial anthology of waka from Heian period, and the first to include *tanrenga* ("short linked verse", composed by two poets), the earliest form of renga recorded.

Sōgi (Iio o Inō Sōgi; 1421–1502): born of a humble family, he is considered the greatest master of renga (linked verse) —in Sōgi's day, renga was cultivated by the warrior class as well as by courtiers, while he was born a commoner. Buddhist monk, in his 30s he became a professional renga poet, known as a traveler-poet.

Tanka: a genre of classical Japanese poetry (see Waka) of thirty-one *on* (sound units) in two stanzas —called respectively *'kami-no-ku'* ("upper phrase"), of 5-7-5 'on', and *'shimo-no-ku'* ("lower phrase"), of 7-7 'on'. Originally, the term tanka meant "short poem", as opposed to 'chōka' ("long poem"). Notably with the compilation of the Kokinshū (at the beginning of 10th century), the short poem became the dominant form of poetry, and the general word 'waka' became the term used to name it. The term tanka was then revived by Masaoka Shiki —end of 19th century.

Taishō period: (1912–1926), is considered the time of the liberal movement known as the "Taishō democracy" in Japan, and is usually distinguished from the preceding Meiji period and the following militarism-driven first part of the Shōwa period.

Teitoku Matsunaga (1571–1653): poet credited as the founder of haikai (he was excluded from the highest levels of waka training because he was a commoner).

Tenja: judge or 'marker' —the master who gave grades to students/competitors.

Tentori haikai: point-garnering haikai (as a profitable business), with masters grading the compositions submitted by their students.

Tokugawa: the last shogunate in Japan (1603–1867), founded by Tokugawa Ieyasu (1543–1616). The shogunate was followed by the restoration of imperial power (see also: Edo period; Meiji period).

Tsukeku: capping stanza in haikai poetry.

Tsukubashū: "The Tsukuba Anthology", the first imperial anthology of renga, compiled c. 1356 (Muromachi period).

Tsurayuki Ki no: (872–945), waka poet and the principal compiler of the Kokin Wakashū, the first imperially-sponsored anthology of waka poetry; in the introduction he named six poets who, later on, were called the "six poetry immortals" ("Rokkasen").

Ukiyo (the floating world): an ideal world of fashion, popular entertainment, and the discovery of aesthetic qualities in objects and actions of everyday life (sort of "hedonistic lifestyle" of the merchant class in Edo period).

Ukiyo-e: ("pictures of the floating world") a genre of woodblock prints and paintings depicting subjects from everyday life, that flourished from the (late) 17th through 19th centuries.

Ushin: depth of feeling.

Utakai Hajime: annual gathering, convened by the Emperor of Japan, in which participants read tanka poetry on a common theme —any poet whose work is selected is invited to attend. It is held on January 1st at the Tokyo Imperial Palace, and broadcast live on the national television network.

Utakotoba: the standard poetic diction, with a sound unit counts of 5–7–5 and

7–7 'on', as established in the *Kokin Wakashū* (Kokinshū, beginning of 900).

Utamakura ("poem pillow"): making reference to historical events or places, like locations familiar to the court of ancient Japan, to allow greater allusions and achieve yugen (mystery and depth) by adding profundity. It was broadly used in waka and renga poetry [see also *'Makura kotoba'* ("pillow words")].

Wabi: patina, rustic beauty and loneliness; subdued, austere beauty.

Wabi-sabi: beauty in simplicity.

Waka: ("Japanese poem") up to and during the compilation of the *Man'yōshū* (c. 760), it was a general term for poetry composed in Japanese, and included several genres such as *tanka* ("short poem"), *chōka* ("long poem"), *bussokusekika* ("Buddha footprint poem") and *sedōka* ("repeating-the-first-part poem"). Later on, by the time of the Kokinshū's compilation (beginning of 900), the word waka became synonymous with tanka, since sedōka, bussokusekika and other forms had gone extinct, while chōka had significantly diminished in prominence. For this reason, the word tanka fell out of use, until the end of the 19th century, when Masaoka Shiki revived it.

Yūgen: depth and mystery; mysterious profundity.

Zōka: the creative force of nature.

pressing my breasts

with both hands

I kick open the door

to mystery

a flower in dark red

Yosano Akiko (1878–1942)
(translated by Makoto Ueda)

ABOUT THE POETS

Anna Banasiak, Poland

— Born in Poland in 1984, I live in Łódź, in the central part of the Country. I studied Polish philology at the University of Warsaw and occupational therapy at the University of Humanities and Economics in Lodz. I'm an occupational therapist by profession; a poet and writer. The winner of poetry competitions in London, Berlin and Bratislava, my poetry can be found in most of the Anthologies published by F. Frosini & PUW. I published a book for children ("Opowieści z Krainy Os", 2017; in Polish), and a book of poems ("Duet of Waves", JUNPA BOOKS, 2018; in English and Japanese, with Yoshimasa Kanou).

~*~

Simon J. Daniel, India

— I am Indian by birth: Simon is my first name; family name, Daniel. Born in 1968, I'm currently resident in Guntur, Andhra Pradesh, where I am a faculty Associate Professor in English at KL University.

~*~

Sheryl Deane, South Africa

— Born 1963, I live in Cape Town, South Africa. A musician and Concert Organiser by profession, I write in my spare time. I completed my studies in English and Music at the University of Natal, KZN, South Africa, where I obtained a B.Mus (Hons). My father and mother read me many poems as a child, including poems by Wordsworth, Blake, Keats, Yates and TS Eliot: it became a way of thinking from an early age. I started to write after my father died. My poetry is inspired by modern poets like Ted Hughes, Olive Schreiner and Bessie Head. Writers such as Roald Dahl, C SLewis, Terry Pratchet are a favourite inspiration. My short story, "Time to Jump", won first Prize in a Whisper Poetry 2016 edition.

~*~

Fabrizio Frosini, Italy

— Born in Tuscany in 1953, and currently living close to Florence, I'm the author of over 3,000 poems and a few short stories, published in 30 personal collections. I'm the founder of the International Association "Poets Unite, Worldwide." Author's Page: https://www.amazon.com/Fabrizio-Frosini/e/B014HA8ZUA/

~*~

Nicholas Gill, UK

— Born in 1963, Nicholas has spent most of his working life as a jazz piano player specialising in vintage styles. He performs anywhere from music festivals to retirement homes and open air markets. As well as developing a piano style, over the last 30 years he has also written poetry to express his own feelings and observations, as well as painting a broader, more universal picture of the Human Condition. He has so far published one volume entitled "Always of the River" in 2015.

~*~

Carlo C. Gomez, USA

— Born in 1970, I live in Southern California, with my beloved wife of 26 years. I have been trained in public speaking for nearly thirty years and teach others to master the ability. I also enjoy photography as a hobby. You can find my poetry on hellopoetry.

~*~

Birgitta Abimbola Heikka, USA

— I was born in Lagos, Nigeria, in 1960 (the year of "equality" for many African countries), to a Swedish father and a Nigerian mother. I moved to the U.S. in 1987. I'm currently living in the state of Maryland. I have two wonderful daughters. My book at Amazon: https://www.amazon.com/Birgitta-Life-Wired-Abimbola-Heikka/dp/1589098919/

~*~

Lidia Hristeva, UK

— I was born a sheep in the Chinese year of 1955 in the ancient city of Philipopolis, Bulgaria. Nowadays its name is Plovdiv. Thracians, Byzantines, Romans, Ottomans have all left their imprints in this beautiful charming place, raised on seven hills. Ancient history was much appealing to me since youth. I was a dynamic child, involved in all sorts of activities except creative writing. I have been working all my life as a paediatrician, serving the most beautiful and inspirational race on Earth — our children. I use "scribotherapy" to reflect on human existence and life in a parallel reality.

~*~

A. Nadeem Ishaque, USA

— I was born in Karachi, Pakistan, in 1962 and lived there until moving to the United States to pursue a doctorate. I am now settled in the Upstate New York area, and have dual citizenship (US and Pakistan). An electrical engineer/physicist by training, I have diverse interests beyond my scientific pursuits ranging from philosophy and literature to art and architecture. In the past I've written philosophical essays, literary criticism and architecture criticism, but started writing poetry only recently in my mid-fifties. I am a devotee of early-to-mid-century modernism in architecture, art, music and literature exemplified by Eliot and Baudelaire in poetry and Leos Janacek in music.

~*~

Joji Varghese Kuncheria, India (currently in UAE)

— I'm an Indian national, a world citizen rather, presently living in Abu Dhabi, UAE. I was born in Kerala, India, in 1953 (a few years after the independence). I started my career as a teacher in Ethiopia at the age of 25 and worked for 42 years, in four different countries, before retiring lately. Poetry is more like a hobby for me, though I had been a keen player of hockey, bridge and chess in my yester years. I respect everyone's personal religious belief that promotes peace and harmony. I'm very passionate about the peaceful co-existence of the people everywhere in this planet, and cherish to see such a world order in the years to come.

~*~

Konstantinos Lagos, Greece

— My name is fr. Konstantinos Lagos. I was born in Athens, in 1978. I am a Greek Orthodox priest, currently serving in Athens, after a few years in the isle of Kithera (a big island with a few inhabitants). The first verse I wrote was for a high school heavy-metal band. Unfortunately the band never got famous and neither did I. When I discovered haiku poetry it was like finding El Dorado. So many feelings and pictures in just three lines and seventeen syllables.. So here I am! Cheers to you all; God bless! My blogs: https://poihsh-palh.blogspot.gr/ (poetic wrestling) and https://tragoudiglarou.blogspot.gr/ (song of the seagull).

~*~

Aron Cheruiyot Lelei, Kenya

— I am a Kenyan poet born in 1968. I come from the Kipsigis sub-tribe of the greater Kalenjin tribe, in Londiani, Kericho County of Central Rift Valley: this is the green land of Kenya and the place I call home. I'm currently living in Nairobi; married to a beautiful queen, we are blest with two boys and one girl. I have the passion of writing and poetry is my favourite way to express myself.

~*~

Mark J. (Mj) Lemon, Canada

— Born in 1963, I am a Canadian, living in British Columbia. I have published over the years, and now turn to poetry to reconnect with the past.

~*~

Geeta Radhakrishna Menon, India

— Born 1950 in Mumbai, Geeta is a Mohiniattam danseuse, Sopanam singer, Yoga practitioner and a Poetess. As a dancer-choreographer, she has performed in various parts of India and other countries —among them: England, Switzerland, France, Nederland, Germany, Luxembourg, Belgium, Sri Lanka, USA, Russia and China. Academically, she is a B.Sc, LL.B, and Ph.D in Philosophy (Thesis: "Narayane-eyam: Philosophy, Bhakti and Aesthetics"). So far, Dr. Geeta has authored 10 books on varied topics, and published a series of Dance, Music & Talk shows at You Tube, while her poems can be found at PoemHunter. Dr. Geeta also specialised in singing the Sopanam style of Kerala Music. She lives in Mumbai (Maharashtra).

~*~

Valsa George Nedumthallil, India

— Born in 1953, I live in a suburb of Ernakulam, Kerala (in the south-west of India), where I lead a happy and contented life. After a successful career as a college teacher, when I retired from service, I took to poetry which I find is a fruitful way of spending time. I write on a wide spectrum of topics spanning Nature, Love and Human relations. My poems have appeared in several journals and magazines of national repute. I have to my credit, four published volumes of poems: 'Beats', 'Drop of a Feather', 'Entwining Shadows' and 'Rainbow Hues', the latter two available on Amazon.com. One of my poems, 'A space Odyssey', is included in the CBSC syllabus for the 8th grade students in India (2018-2020). Another poem, 'My Fractured Identity', is prescribed for the undergraduate students (Voyagers) in the country of Philippines. Through my poems, I try to assert that despite the sham, chaos and confusion, life is beautiful and worth living.

~*~

275

Mohammed Asim Nehal, India

— Born 1969 and brought up in Nagpur (Maharashtra), the 'orange city' of India, I started writing poetry and short stories at a very young age. I feel poetry as a trick of language that magnetizes the readers and takes them to a world that is virtually created by the poets. By profession, I am a Chartered Accountant and a Company Secretary with Master's degree in Commerce and Bachelor's degree in Law. What I studied for and what I feel are two parallel lines.

~*~

Namita Rani Panda, India

— Born 1965, I am a multilingual poet, story writer and translator from Sambalpur of Odisha, India. Currently living in Cuttack, I work as Vice-Principal of Jawahar Navodaya Vidyalaya, under the Ministry of HRD, Dept. of School Education and Literacy, Govt. of India. I have five solo anthologies of poems to my credit: Blue Butterflies, Rippling Feelings, A Slice of Sky, A Song for Myself, and Colours of Love. I have co-authored Rivulets of Reflections, a book of translated stories. My signature words are love, optimism and self-confidence. I am an active member of 'Cosmic Crew', a literary group of female poets of Odisha working with the motto "My pen for the world." I am editor of 'Radical Rhythm-2', an anthology of poems by Cosmic Crew.

~*~

Annette Potgieter, South Africa

— I was born in Belgium in 1973 to South African parents. After spending my childhood in various European countries, my parents returned to South Africa in 1991. I have studied Industrial and Organisational Psychology and am a Human Resource Manager by profession. Poetry is a language my soul understands. And though silence is a treasured friend, my love is written words. I live in Pretoria.

~*~

Udaya R. Tennakoon, Switzerland

— My full name is Udaya Rathna Tennakoon Mudiyanselage. As a Diaspora Poet, I live in Zürich, Switzerland, but my home country is Sri Lanka, where I was born in 1970. A political refugee, I can see the world from many perspectives and engage through writing and research. I graduated from University of Colombo and University of Kelaniya, Sri Lanka. At the University of Basel, Switzerland, and also at the University of Innsbruck, Austria, I studied 'Peace and Conflict Transformation' for my master's degree. As a writer, I compose for the theater and contribute articles to many websites. I am also a social activist and I engage with many volunteer organizations in Switzerland and Europe as well as in Nepal and Sri Lanka. In 2017 I published a book of haiku titled 'The Fragrance of Loss'.

~*~

Hans Van Rostenberghe, Malaysia

— Born 1964, in Oudenaarde, Belgium, I'm currently living in a town called Bachok, in Kelantan State, Malaysia. I am a doctor in medicine (neonatologist) and a professor at Universiti Sains Malaysia, where I have been working since 1994. Among the most important sources of inspiration in my life are Dr. Albert Schweitzer, Dr. Martin Luther King and the Organization 'Médécins sans Frontieres'. Poetry has become a passion since 2010, and I write under the pseudonym 'Aufie Zophy'. I am a reader of philosophy, a nature lover and a family man. I believe strongly that the world is heading towards harmony through an ever increasing kindness revolution which is close to its sharp inflection point on its exponential curve. I express my ideas in short essays and poems. My blog: 'Soul sprinkles', http://reflectionsbyhans.blogspot.com/.

~*~

Steven R. Vogel, USA

— I began writing and performing music and poetry not many years after my birth in 1956. I've lived in three distinct regions of the United States (west of the Mississippi—much of it ON the Mississippi—Minnesota presently) and have worked and written on farms, in villages, in midsized cities, and in suburban and metropolitan areas. I have served in medicine and the academy for more than three decades.

~*~

Caroline Watsham, UK

— Caroline Watsham hails from the South of England, where she lives on a colourful and chaotic narrowboat on a rural canal with her three cats. She is also a proud mother of two adult daughters. By day she supports young disabled adults and children in a special (in every sense) school in Oxfordshire. In her spare time she is drawn to the artistic and the unusual: she is an accomplished musical saw player (amongst other instruments), and also loves to act, sing and create various forms of art. She draws inspiration from ancient forms of spirituality and timeless human emotions.

~*~

Somayeh Zare, Iran

— My name is Somayeh but people call me Sarah. I was born in England in 1991, but my family returned to Iran when I was still a little child. I currently live in Karaj, a city close to Tehran, and have an M.Sc. in medical biotechnology. As far as I remember, I have always been fascinated by the world of poetry and fiction, so I started writing poetry in my native language, Persian. However, I didn't want to limit myself to one language when it comes to poetry —that's why when a friend suggested I join PUW, I did it without thinking twice. I still have a lot to learn as a poet, but I want my heart to guide me in the art of Poetry. I really appreciate being accepted as a new member of this group.

our life in this world

is like the image one sees

inside a mirror —

something that's not really there,

but then not really not-there

Minamoto no Sanetomo (1192–1219)
(translated by Steven D. Carter)

Poets Unite Worldwide

'Poets Unite Worldwide' represents, in my mind, an invitation and an appeal (*"Poets worldwide, unite!"*), and it is more an open group of poets, an independent community, than a formal association —but still an 'Association' of over two hundred free minds and spirits.

I'd say that this comes, first, from my own nature: I consider myself not just an Italian, but a Citizen of the World —*born in Italy by chance*—, equal to everybody else: all human beings on planet Earth, in brotherhood. I have an independent mind and the utmost respect for the human values of *freedom, justice, privacy..* and I dislike almost all kind of formalities: for such reason I stay away from anything that sounds bureaucratic.

Although living in different countries and continents, we all feel a kinship, being part of this poetic drive for worldwide peace and brotherhood. In such a way, we work together for the highest purposes, as all mankind should do.

I can say that 'Poets Unite Worldwide' was born, in its extended form, in the Autumn of 2015, when I invited scores of poets, worldwide, to join me in writing a poetry compilation on (against) terror, in response to the bloody Paris events of November 13, 2015.

I felt the urge, that time, to began working on a new ebook, '**Poetry Against Terror**', and I enlisted 'my' community of poets worldwide to help, since I wanted it to become a large collective work: the voice of poets from many different countries, worldwide, who stand up and speak aloud, but without hatred, against the bloody madness of terror. Astonishingly, 64 Poets from 43 countries lent their pens in the effort, and I wrote, in the introductory note to the book, "*we—poets of the world—wish to make our voices resonate in the minds and hearts of all women and men who refuse to be silenced by hate and violence.*" Pamela Sinicrope and Daniel Brick, both of Minnesota, USA, along with Richard Thézé, England, co-edited the collection of diverse poems about terrorism —in Paris and around the world. Cover art was by Galina Italyanskaya, Russia.

The project came together quickly, with poets coming from countries in all continents, including Arab/Islamic countries: *Australia, Bangladesh, Botswana, Brazil, Canada, Chile, China, Croatia, Egypt, France, Germany, Ghana, Greece, India, Indonesia, Iran, Ireland, Israel, Italy, Kenya, Morocco, New Zealand , Nepal, Nigeria, Oman, Pakistan, Philippines, Qatar, Russia, Saudi Arabia, Serbia, Somalia, South Africa, Sri Lanka, Sweden, Switzerland, Thailand, Tunisia, United Arab Emirates, Uganda, United Kingdom, USA, Zimbabwe.*

Poem topics range from a focus on the liberty of France, to the musings of a mother who does not want her child suffering from terrorism, to a young woman who incessantly searches Google for the answers to the terrorism problem, to the story of African villagers who drink from a cow's horn under a peaceful moon until terrorism takes over. Many of the poets have experienced terrorism first-hand, and this witness is expressed in their writings and their biographies. As Pamela Sinicrope said, "*We've all been touched by terrorism. For some, the topic hit home after the events in Paris, but for others, terrorism has been a disturbing part of everyday life —these facts are borne out in the poems. The poems speak for themselves."*

Yet, as a group of poets collaborating together on a variety of projects, we didn't stop with that first book. We do have a blog, that Udaya Tennakon created, as well as a Fb page (see below). Since then, we've been continually publishing and growing, and –hopefully– improving as writers.

In Spring 2016 we published the ebook **'Poets Against Inequality'**, to add our voice to those other unequivocal voices that denounce an absolute lack of equality in our society. The poems collected in that book (as well as the previous one) belong in what is called "*Poetry of Witness*", and we believe that this is a task that all of us, as poets, have a moral obligation to pursue, because we can't accept to live in a world where extreme poverty is so widespread and sheer inequality is the norm.

Another project accomplished is a book on the Refugees theme: in March 2016, while looking at an image taken on the border between Greece and Macedonia, I felt the urge to write a poem. From that urge, a new editorial project was born (the book **'By Land & By Seas'**); then many others followed, like **'We All Are Persons – Why Gender Discrimination?'**, or '**Time to show up – Poetry for Democracy**', or **'Our Only World – Poetry for Planet Earth'**, about our endangered world. Up to now, we've published over 60 books, and surely, thanking the enthusiasm and energy of many in our group, new good projects will follow. Our mission keeps on.

Fabrizio Frosini
(*on behalf of 'Poets Unite Worldwide'*)

Our Facebook Page: https://www.facebook.com/poetsuniteworldwide/
Our Website: https://poetsuniteworldwide.org/

Other books from the same Publisher

*(**BE**: Bilingual Editions, English–Italian — translated into Italian by F. Frosini)*
(All books have both a PAPERBACK and an EBOOK Edition)

POETRY:

– 'At The Crossing Of Seven Winds' – English Ed.;
– 'Nine Tales Of Creation' – English Ed.;
– 'Scattering Dreams & Tales' – English Ed.;
– 'We Are The Words – Siamo Parole' – ***BE***;
– 'Whispers to the World – Sussurri al Mondo" – ***BE***;
– 'How to write Poetry, A Handbook – Come scrivere Poesie, Manuale'– ***BE***;
– 'Poetry Against Terror'– English Ed.;
– 'Poets Against Inequality'– English Ed.;
– 'By Land & By Seas – Poetry for the Refugees' – English Ed.;
– 'We All Are Persons – Why Gender Discrimination?' – English Ed.;
– 'United We Stand – Poets Against Terror' – English Ed.;
– 'A Note, a Word, a Brush – Ode to the Arts' – English Ed.;
– 'Voices without veils' – English Ed.;
– 'Our Chains, Our Dreams' [Part One] – English Ed.;
– 'Our Chains, Our Dreams' [Part Two] – English Ed.;
– 'Our Chains, Our Dreams' [Part Three] – English Ed.;
– 'Singing Together – Poems for Christmas' – English Ed.;
– 'Let's Laugh Together – Poems for Children' – English Ed.;
– 'Children We Are — Poems for Children' – English Ed.;
– 'From an Old Path – Contemporary European Poetry' – English Ed.;
– 'Tunes from the Indian Subcontinent – Contemporary Poetry' – English Ed.;
– 'Whispering to the Heart – Contemporary African Poetry' – English Ed.;
– 'Hues of the World – Contemporary Poetry' – English Ed.;
– 'The Sounds of America – Contemporary American Poetry' – English Ed.;
– 'Poems from a Land of Wonders' – English Ed.;
– 'Fifty-six Female Voices of Contemporary Poetry' – English Ed.;
– 'The Feminine Heart of Poetry' – English Ed.;
– 'Spring Songs' – English Ed.;
– 'Summer Arias' – English Ed.;
– 'Autumn Lullabies' – English Ed.;
– 'Winter Melodies' – English Ed.;
– 'The Four Seasons Poetry Concerto' – English Ed.;
– 'Glimmers of Light–Guizzi di Luce' – T. Billsborough & F. Frosini – ***BE***;

– 'The Soprano of Sunlight–Luce di Soprano' – Billsborough, Frosini – ***BE***;
– 'Faith is the Fifth Dimension' – Billsborough, Frosini – English Ed.;
– 'Marie & Josephine – A long poem' – Tom Billsborough – English Ed.;
– 'The Double Door' by Daniel J. Brick & Fabrizio Frosini – English Ed.;
– 'Through Time, Through Space' – English Ed.;
– 'Geography & Music of Poetry' – English Ed.;
– 'Space of the Mind' – English Ed.;
– 'From the Past to the Future' – English Ed.;
– 'When Love is Bitter' – English Ed.;
– 'Abstract Life, Abstract Love' – English Ed.;
– 'About Love' – English Ed.;
– 'Seasons of the Fleeting World – Writing Haiku' – English Ed.;
– 'Moments of Lightness – Haiku & Tanka' – English Ed.;
– 'Born on a Full Moon — Senryū' – English Ed.;
– 'One Step At A Time' – English Ed.;
– 'The Moon & The Humans' – English Ed.;
– 'Homo Homini Lupus: Why To kill a Mockingbird?' – English Ed.;
– 'About Abel & Cain —or The Best & Worst of Human Society' – English Ed.;
– 'Quis custodiet ipsos custodes? — The wave of global protest' – English Ed.;
– 'Time to show up – Poetry for Democracy' – English Ed.;
– 'In the Name of Democracy: Poetic Voices' – English Ed.;
– 'The Beauty of Diversity — Racial Prejudice, A Moral Shame' – English Ed.;
– 'Our Only World – Poetry for Planet Earth' – English Ed.;
– 'A Disconsolate Planet — Poems on Climate Emergency' – English Ed.;
– 'What Planet For Our Grandchildren?' – English Edition.
– 'The Healing Power of Poetry — Poems in the Time of Pandemic' – English Ed.;
– 'Poetic Fantasies' Vol. 1. – English Ed.;
– 'Poetic Fantasies' Vol. 2. – English Ed.;
– 'Poetic Fantasies' Vol. 3. – English Ed.;
– 'Poetic Fantasies' Vol. 4. – English Ed.;
– 'Poetic Fantasies' Vol. 5. – English Ed.;
– 'A Christmas with Us — Poems & Tales for Christmas' – English Ed.;
– 'Witty Moments — Poetry Anthology' – English Ed.;
– 'Family is Forever — Poems' – English Ed.;
– *'Tiptoeing In & Out — Tanka' – English Edition.*

FICTION & ESSAYS:

– 'Essays on the World of Humans' – D.J. Brick & F. Frosini – English Ed.;
– 'Harry Buoy–A Novel' – Tom Billsborough – English Ed.;
– 'Short Tales Extravaganza' – English Ed.;
– 'Whispers in the Twilight — Short Stories' – English Ed.;

– 'The Realm of The Mind — Fairy Tales Collection' – English Ed.;
– 'Grains of Sand — Short Stories' – English Edition.

FORTHCOMING PUBLICATIONS:

– *'Poetic Fantasies' Vol. 6. – English Edition.*

Books by Fabrizio Frosini as sole Author

POETRY:

– «The Chinese Gardens – English Poems» – English Ed. – (published also in Italian Ed.:
– «I Giardini Cinesi» – Edizione Italiana);
– «KARUMI – Haiku & Tanka» – Italian Ed.;
– «Allo Specchio di Me Stesso» ('In the Mirror of Myself') – Italian Ed.;
– «Il Vento e il Fiume» ('The Wind and the River') – Italian Ed.;
– «A Chisciotte» ('To Quixote') – Italian Ed.;
– «Il Puro, l'Impuro – Kosher/Treyf» ('The pure, the Impure – Kosher / Treyf') – Italian Ed.;
– «Frammenti di Memoria – Carmina et Fragmenta» ('Fragments of Memories') – Italian Ed.;
– «La Città dei Vivi e dei Morti» ('The City of the Living and the Dead') – Italian Ed.;
– «Nella luce confusa del crepuscolo» ('In the fuzzy light of the Twilight') – Italian Ed.;
– «Limes —O La Chiave Dei Sogni» ('The Key to Dreams') – Italian Ed.;
– «Echi e Rompicapi» ('Puzzles & Echoes') – Italian Ed.;
– «Ballate e Altre Cadenze» ('Ballads and Other Cadences') – Italian Ed.;
– «Selected Poems – Επιλεγμένα Ποιήματα – Poesie Scelte» – Greek–English–Italian (Αγγλικά, Ελληνικά, Ιταλικά – Greek translation by Dimitrios Galanis);
– «Prelude to the Night – English Poems» – English Ed. (published also in Italian Ed.:
– «Preludio alla Notte» – Edizione Italiana);
– «A Season for Everyone – Tanka Poetry» – English Ed.;
– «Evanescence of the Floating World – Haiku» – English Ed.;
– «From the Book of Limbo – Dal Libro del Limbo» – *BE*;
– «Anita Quiclotzl & Her Souls – Anita Quiclotzl e le Sue Anime» – *BE*;
– «La Casa Fatta di Foglie — Poesie» ('A House Made of Leaves') – Italian Ed.;
– «Interior of a Pulsar — Poems» – English Ed. – (published also in Italian Ed.:
– «Interno di una Pulsar — Poesie»);
– «Di lato alla Luna — Poesie» ('Sideways to the Moon') – Italian Ed.;

FICTION:

– «Mirror Games — A Tale» – English Edition (also in Italian Ed.:
– «Giochi di Specchi — Un Racconto»);
– «The Visitor – A Winter Tale» – English Edition (also in Italian Ed.:
– «Il Visitatore – Racconto d'Inverno»);
– «The Great Valley – A children's story» – English Ed. (also in Italian Ed.:

– «La Grande Valle – Racconto per ragazzi»).

FORTHCOMING PUBLICATIONS:

– *«Racconti Sciolti Sparsi – Scattered Loose Tales» – *BE*;*
– *«Topicality of Limen – Poems» – English Ed. – (also in Italian Ed.:*
– *«Attualità del Limen – Poesie»).*

Publisher's Page at Amazon

https://www.amazon.com/Fabrizio-Frosini/e/B014HA8ZUA/

~*~

Poets Unite Worldwide

Our Fb page

https://www.facebook.com/poetsuniteworldwide/

Our web-site

https://poetsuniteworldwide.org/